**W9-CXP-838**

# Invasive Aquatic and Wetland Plants

# INVASIVE SPECIES

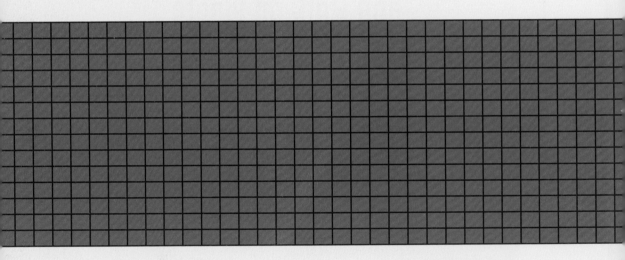

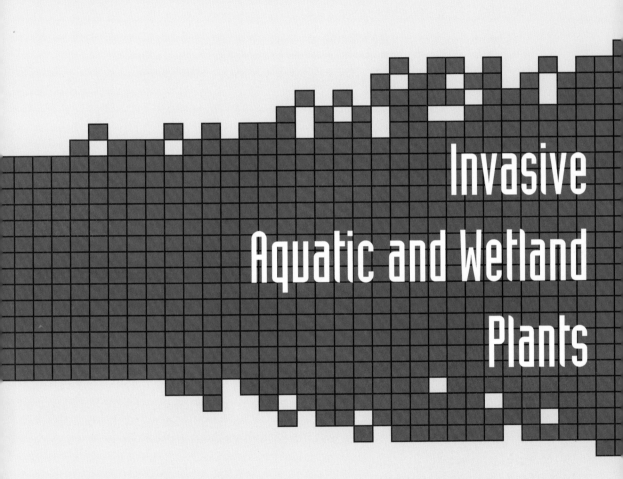

# Invasive Aquatic and Wetland Plants

## Suellen May

CHELSEA HOUSE
PUBLISHERS
An imprint of Infobase Publishing

**Invasive Aquatic and Wetland Plants**

Copyright © 2007 by Infobase Publishing

Chelsea House
An imprint of Infobase Publishing
132 West 31st Street
New York NY 10001

**Library of Congress Cataloging-in-Publication Data**

May, Suellen.
  Invasive aquatic and wetland plants / Suellen May.
     p. cm. — (Invasive species)
  Includes bibliographical references and index.
  ISBN 0-7910-9130-9 (hardcover)
1. Aquatic weeds—Juvenile literature. 2. Invasive plants—Juvenile literature. I. Title.
II. Series: May, Suellen. Invasive species.
  SB614.M41 2006
  581.7'6—dc22

                          2006009054

Chelsea House books are available at special discounts when purchased in bulk quantities for businesses, associations, institutions, or sales promotions. Please call our Special Sales Department in New York at (212) 967-8800 or (800) 322-8755.

You can find Chelsea House on the World Wide Web at http://www.chelseahouse.com

Text design by James Scotto-Lavino
Cover design by Takeshi Takahashi

Printed in the United States of America

Bang FOF 10 9 8 7 6 5 4 3 2 1

This book is printed on acid-free paper.

All links and Web addresses were checked and verified to be correct at the time of publication. Because of the dynamic nature of the Web, some addresses and links may have changed since publication and may no longer be valid.

# TABLE OF CONTENTS

# What Are Aquatic and Wetland Plants?

1

• • • • • • • • • • • • • • • • • • • • • • • • • •

**A**quatic plants, or hydrophytes, are plants that are bound to the water to complete their life cycle. They can be herbaceous or woody and at least some portion of the plant grows in water. Herbaceous plants have soft tissues and do not develop woody parts aboveground. Some aquatic plants are completely submerged and others grow just along the water's edge.

Aquatic vegetation is further categorized as either a macrophyte or microphyte. A macrophyte is a plant that can be viewed without a microscope. Aquatic macrophytes are a diverse group of flowering plants, mosses, ferns, and macroalgae (large algae) that make the water their home. Microphytes are unicellular, meaning that they have only one cell.

Aquatic and wetland plants provide habitats for fish, invertebrates, amphibians, and waterfowl as well as mammals. These plants provide oxygen and a place for aquatic life to reproduce. Their roots, stems, and leaves protect streams, riverbanks, and shorelines. Temperature and light are stabilized as a result of this plant growth. Proper nutrient recycling and slowing of sediment transport are also critical functions of wetland and aquatic plants.

Similar to terrestrial (land) plants, aquatic and wetland plants produce food through photosynthesis. Aquatic and wetland plants make their own food by converting light energy to chemical energy. Most plants store this energy as food in the bonds of sugar or starch.

The aquatic environment is less varied than terrestrial environments that include deserts, forests, grasslands, and tundra. In some ways, an aquatic environment is easier for plants in terms of water availability, temperatures, and nutrient bathing. However, there are challenges that plants face in an aquatic environment.

Plants need oxygen and carbon dioxide to live. Aquatic plants have a more difficult time getting these because the gases dissolve more slowly in water than in air. Aquatic vegetation needs light to photosynthesize, but light can be blocked by an aquatic plant canopy or by sediments in the water.

The aquatic environment has advantages over terrestrial biomes. (A biome is a region characterized by similar climate, soil, plants, and animals.) Anyone who swims is aware of the buoyancy of water. Aquatic plants need less support tissue as a result, saving energy that can be used for other plant functions. In terrestrial plants, nutrient absorption occurs primarily through the roots. However, in submersed plants, the leaves can act as roots by absorbing nutrients.

## WHERE AQUATIC PLANTS LIVE

The following allegory helps explain in symbolic terms the complexity of aquatic plant systems. A young ecologist thought he found a way to decipher the coral reef. He believed that all he needed to do was feed the data about reefs into a huge supercomputer, type a few commands, push the Enter key, and out would come the secrets of life on the reef. He gave it a whirl. What issued from the computer was not the reef's intricately drawn food web that the scientist had hoped to reveal, but billowing clouds of smoke. Presented with such an impossible task, the supercomputer had blown up.[1] This story illustrates the point that coral reefs are so complicated that humans cannot come close to predicting every variable that contributes to the function of biological communities. These complexities are not limited to coral reefs, however. For as little as is understood about the reefs, even more is left to discover about other aquatic environments.

The obvious distinction when it comes to aquatic vegetation is whether the environment is freshwater or marine (salt water). A variety of habitats exist within salt and fresh waters.

## Oceans

The evolution of life began in the sea. All living creatures need water. Plants made the move to land by re-creating their wet environment and sealing it within themselves.[2] A tree has a large underground network of roots that bring water from the soil into the tree's main structure. Water is vital to life and where there is more water, plant life tends to flourish.

It comes as no surprise then that the ocean rivals the rain forests in terms of biological diversity. The deep sea, 3,250 feet (1,000 meters) and more beneath the surface of the ocean, was previously thought to be lifeless, only to be discovered to be so rich with biological diversity that now it is referred to as an unexplored continent.

Dredging of this ocean floor in the 1960s revealed swarms of worms, crustaceans, mollusks, and other animals found nowhere else on Earth. At the sea bottom alone, there is no way of knowing the total number of species, but estimates for animal species range in the tens of millions. The diversity of bacteria and other microorganisms cannot even be guessed to order of magnitude.[3] In addition to being home to a rich complex of aquatic life, oceans support terrestrial life by serving as a reservoir of dissolved carbon dioxide that regulates carbon dioxide in the atmosphere.

The percentage of salt is an important indicator of species distribution, particularly where freshwater and salt-water habitats intermingle. The proportion of different chemicals in seawater is amazingly constant in all the world's seas, but the total quantity of dissolved salts varies.[4] The percentage of salt in the open sea is about 35%. Waters closer to the coast approach 32%. It doesn't sound like much of a difference, but it alters the types of species found there as much as the species found between desert and grassland.

Oceans cover 71% of the Earth's surface, and of this vast area three habitats comprise the ocean biome: pelagic, balanoid-thallophyte, and pelecypod-annelid. A **pelagic** habitat consists of plants and animals that float or drift free in the open sea. The other two marine biomes are benthic, where organisms crawl, creep, burrow, or attach themselves to the ocean bottom or to each other. Benthic plants must live where the water is shallow so that they can receive light and therefore photosynthesize (Figure 1.1).[5]

**Balanoid-thallophyte** is another type of habitat where members need something to attach to, such as a rocky shore. Although this term may be a mouthful, it is easy to understand if you know the meaning of each of the terms. **Balanoid** refers to barnacles. **Thallophyte** refers to plants that absorb their food over a growing surface, such as a rocky shore.

The balanoid-thallophyte habitat can be easily observed. Have you ever seen what looks like foamy bathtub rings along the coastline? These are intertidal zones where the water line varies between high and low tides. Barnacles and seaweeds are common in this habitat, as well as brightly colored lichen that appear above the water zone and are tolerant of occasional mists of salt water.

The **pelecypod-annelid** biome consists of unconsolidated sediments. This term can be better understood when the terms are defined. **Pelecypod** refers to animals that have a shell, such as a clam. **Annelid** refers to animals that have a segmented body, such as a leech. Unconsolidated sediments are soft grounds with varying textures depending on particle size and are then classified as sand, silt, or clay. Many of the organisms that live here are burrowers, such as worms.

Temperature is another factor that affects the distribution of species. From the surface of a placid pond to the arctic depths of the ocean's abyss, temperature varies with depth, latitude, and season. Temperature variations alter species and force change and competition in their environment.

Similar to lakes and ponds, there is a seasonal changeover in oceans where the warmer top layer of the ocean mixes with the much colder bottom layer. A zone of steeply decreasing temperature called a thermocline separates the extreme

**Figure 1.1** The ocean biome covers the majority of the Earth's surface. This species-rich system contains a variety of life-forms from floating plankton to benthic creatures burrowing deep in the ocean floor sediment.

temperature variations in the top and bottom layers. Autumn causes the top layer of water to cool and become heavier, and then the surface and bottom layers begin to mix; the thermocline breaks and the extreme temperature contrast is reduced. Nutrients are brought to the surface and provide a food source for zooplankton (tiny animals that drift with the ocean currents), fish, birds, and on up the food chain.

## Wetlands

In Stone Harbor, New Jersey, the Wetlands Institute is a 6,000-acre preserve of coastal wetlands. As visitors step out of their cars and walk through the manicured gardens, one can't help but inhale deeply the fragrant salt air. Coming quickly into view is the captivating, stark contrast of blue waters set against green vegetation. During the 1960s, before there were many regulations in New Jersey to prevent their destruction, coastal wetlands were disappearing at an astonishing rate. Private and public monies were raised to purchase the land and build the educational center.

A nationally threatened bird of prey, the osprey, returns from its wintering grounds to this area in late March to nest and raise its young. Osprey populations are recovering and growing since the ban of DDT (an insecticide that persisted in the environment) that nearly decimated their populations. The Wetlands Institute is also home to marsh plants, fiddler crabs, great blue herons, and perhaps most proudly, diamondback terrapins, a large species of aquatic turtle. Without the forward-thinking efforts to preserve these acres back in the 1960s, surely this land would have been lost to more casinos and condos that now dominate this area of the New Jersey shore.

Wetlands are the transition environment from land to water. The term refers to marshes, bogs, swamps, and fens. Despite the name, wetlands are not necessarily wet year round; some are only wet for three weeks out of the year. **Marshes** are wetlands dominated by soft-stemmed vegetation. The salt marshes of New Jersey are vast grassy meadows that protect the mainland from flooding, filter sediments and pollutants from the water, and serve as a nursery for many fish and shellfish. Most of the local animals served as seafood in New Jersey spend at least some of the time living in a salt marsh.

Swamps are another type of wetland comprised primarily of woody plants. **Bogs** are freshwater wetlands, often formed in old glacial lakes, characterized by spongy peat deposits, evergreen trees and shrubs, and a floor covered by a thick carpet of sphagnum moss (Figure 1.2). **Fens** are freshwater, peat-forming wetlands covered mostly by grasses, sedges, reeds, and wildflowers. Wetlands are biologically rich with plants and animals. They also provide valuable resting and feeding ground

**Figure 1.2** Bogs differ from other wetlands by the presence of evergreen trees and shrubs. Wetlands are biologically rich and act as a purifier of water. These habitats play a vital role in our environment by providing food, shelter, and breeding grounds for many creatures.

for migrating birds. Degradation of wetlands has been a leading cause of species extinction.

At the Wetlands Institute, salt ponds are shallow depressions in the marsh that are flooded only by high tides, not by the ordinary twice-daily tides. The floor of the salt pond is a thick

## Protecting Our Wetlands

Despite the ecological value of wetlands, the United States loses approximately 60,000 acres of wetlands per year. Although wetlands purify water, pollutants can destroy a wetland. In Florida, the sugarcane industry has been held responsible for polluting and destroying wetlands in the Everglades. Invasive species, both animals and plants, have also been a cause of destruction of wetlands.

State and federal agencies have implemented policies to protect wetlands. One way to protect these lands is to monitor the discharge of pollutants through the issue of permits for residential development, roads, and levees, all of which affect wetlands. Some states will fine polluters of wetlands and require them to compensate for it. New Jersey's Department of Environmental Protection (DEP) reached a settlement with El Paso Corporation, a natural gas transporter, for injuries to wetlands and groundwater at 37 sites in 10 New Jersey counties. As compensation for the damage to the wetlands, El Paso must purchase and preserve 263 wetland acres. In addition, El Paso had to pay New Jersey $260,000 for wetlands restoration work.

Agencies also protect wetlands by prohibiting building on them. Businesses must apply for permits to build, and in many states, alternatives are explored so that construction does not take place on these valuable ecosystems.

layer of silt, mostly from decaying organic materials. These decaying organic materials are a food source for grass shrimp, killifish, and minnows. Few organisms can live here because of the fluctuating salinity levels. Evaporation causes high salt levels whereas flooding and rainwater reduce salinity. The herons,

The Environmental Protection Agency (EPA) is also partnering with states, tribes, and local governments to restore wetlands. The EPA's goal is to increase overall wetlands in the next five years.

Individuals can help protect and restore wetlands. Duck stamps sold in your local post office support the U.S. Fish and Wildlife's efforts to purchase and restore wetlands. When gardening, be aware of possible wetlands; plant native grasses or forested buffer strips along wetlands.

## Create Your Own Wetland

If you already have a wet area in your backyard, creating a wetland may be as simple as selecting wetland plants. If not, choose a natural depression in your backyard with ideally clay soils that will drain slowly. Remember that many wetlands are only wet for a few weeks out of the year and most aren't wet all summer long. If you have a natural depression but it is never wet, you may need to get a plastic or other type of liner. Once plants are established, don't mow or trim this area.

If the area is still too dry, you will need to build a berm (a mound or wall of earth) to hold back water. Go to the United States Department of Agriculture's Natural Resources Conservation Service's Web site to get more specific instructions on creating a wetland.

Source: http://www.nrcs.usda.gov/feature/backyard/BakWet.html.

egrets, ibis, and gulls are grateful for these salt ponds, since the shrimp, minnows, and fish that live here provide a nice snack.

Wetlands are also a great purifier of water by absorbing excess nutrients, sediment, and other pollutants before they reach rivers, lakes, and other water bodies. When rivers overflow, wetlands absorb and slow floodwaters.

## Lakes, Ponds, and Reservoirs

Lakes, ponds, and reservoirs are freshwater. Reservoirs are man-made and, often, so are ponds. Beavers also create ponds by damming streams.

Ponds are shallower than lakes and generally allow light to penetrate the entire depth of the water. Plant life is able to live on the bottom of a pond whereas the bottom of a lake is generally unable to support photosynthesizing plants. In ponds, an ample supply of algae colors the water a healthy dark green. Pond life such as snails, crustaceans, worms, and tadpoles graze on the algae and decaying plant material. Zooplankton feed on algae, bacteria, and other small particles of organic matter.

Tiny plantlike organisms, called **phytoplankton**, green-blue algae, and diatoms are the energy-producing tenants in a lake. Deeper lakes will have more phytoplankton and a greater likelihood of native fish. Although light does not penetrate the entire depth of the lake, species occupy all areas of a lake. In the mucky, dark sediment at the bottom, bloodworms and phantom midge larvae (the young of a tiny fly) feed on falling organic matter. These organisms enrich and stabilize the sediment and help break down bits of plant material not digestible by other animals.

The **littoral zone** is where aquatic, rooted plants grow along a shore or lake (Figure 1.3). It is the area between the highest and lowest tides, also known as the **intertidal** area. The vegetation in this zone behaves similarly to the vegetation in a pond because

**Figure 1.3**  The littoral zone is where rooted plants can live in a body of water. The water is shallow enough for light to penetrate; light is needed by the plants to photosynthesize. Seen here is a littoral zone along the western U.S. coast.

## The Beauty of Pond Scum

Geoscientist Lynn Margulis and her students make a pilgrimage to San Quintin Bay, in Mexico's Baja California Norte, every few years in search of the ecological setting of the earliest cells on Earth. On a lagoon with salt flats, they find laminated, brightly striped sediments underlain by gelatinous mud. These mat-forming algae exist where the sea meets and teases the land. Enchanted, Margulis puts her hands in the mud of fragrant microbial tissues and whiffs the exchanging gases. The smell is akin to rotten eggs. What she smells is death—decaying organic matter—yet the community of algae is very much alive.

Algae consist of three general forms: microscopic, mat-forming, and stonewort. Microscopic algae are typically free floating or attach to rocks and other solid materials in the water. Mat-forming algae are generally considered undesirable because they can become difficult to control once their populations reach high levels. Stonewort algae have simple stem and leaflike structures with a portion embedded in the sediment. Often they become overly abundant in shallow parts of water.

Algae are an important source of oxygen and a primary food source for many aquatic invertebrate animals, such as shellfish. Problems from algae occur when a population crashes or dies off,

the light is able to penetrate the depth of the zone and therefore support plant life.

The littoral zone extends from the water's edge to the maximum water depth where plants can grow in a lake, pond, or reservoir. For oceans, the littoral zone is categorized in more detail. The four transitional zones are the spray zone, high tide zone, middle tide zone, and low tide zone. The **spray zone** or causing the decaying algae to rapidly consume oxygen in the water that is necessary for other organisms.

Algae are chlorophyll-containing organisms, often grouped together in colonies. Algae have been around for more than 2 billion years, and we are still discovering new kinds. Although algae photosynthesize, they are not in the same taxonomic category as plants, that is, Plantae; rather, they are considered protists. Green algae are the most diverse group of all the algae with more than 7,000 species. Algae include pond scums, terrestrial algae, snow algae seaweeds, and freshwater and marine phytoplankton. Unlike plants, algae do not have true leaves or roots.

Some algae use other compounds to store energy. Red algae store energy in the form of floridean starch, and brown algae store energy in the form of laminarin. Since photosynthesis occurs only with the green pigment chlorophyll, this brings into question how these other algae can make their own food when they are not green. They do actually contain the green pigment of chlorophyll but just in smaller amounts that are masked by the red and brown pigments.

Algae do not flower or produce seeds; instead they produce spores for reproduction. These spores are very small, often only one cell, and they are mobile.

upper littoral is dry most of the time. This zone is only wet during extremely high tides or flooding. Cattails, barnacles, and lichen can be found in the spray zone. The **high tide zone** is flooded during high tide. Floating-leaved plants such as water lilies frequently occupy this zone. The **middle tide zone** is covered and uncovered by water daily. The **low tide zone** or **lower littoral** is the deepest part of the water where submersed plants can still grow. This area is exposed only when the tide is extremely low.

As a pond or lake ages, the littoral zone increases. Like most other natural systems, a lake or pond goes through transitional changes over time. This is referred to as **succession.** Succession is the gradual replacement of one set of plant species with another. Succession begins with species that are the first to arrive at an available site and grow relatively quickly without ample nutrients. These species that are first to arrive, usually after a disturbance such as fire, flood, or volcanic eruption, are known as **pioneer species**. Pioneer species alter the environment and make it suitable for the next set of species; they add organic matter, provide shade, and create a varied habitat. As an ecosystem ages, it eventually stops switching out species. This final plant community is known as a **climax community** and indicates a more mature ecosystem. Ponds and lakes change until they reach a climax community, resulting in a larger littoral zone.

## THE ROLE OF AQUATIC AND WETLAND PLANTS

Aquatic and wetland plants provide shelter and food for animals and add oxygen to the water. People rely on the biological richness of aquatic and wetland habitats. We rely on food and other resources from these biological communities or ecosystems. Many other organisms can only survive with plants for food. Animals, microbes (microorganisms), invertebrates (animals without backbones), and plants interact and are dependent on their environment. The term **ecosystem** is used to describe this interdependence where communities of different organisms share and recycle resources needed for maintenance of the community.

Water is a limiting factor in a plant's growth. Aquatic and wetland plants have the fortune of ample access to water, and

**Figure 1.4**   Water lilies float on the surface of the water. They are typical of the kinds of plants that occupy the high tide zone.

they are therefore more productive. It is surprising how much wildlife food is produced in an acre of wetland. In an experiment, scientists found that a plant known as the salt-marsh bulrush, important to overwintering birds in South Carolina, produced an average of about 300 pounds of seeds per acre per year. Seeds are an important source of nutrition for animals but specifically for overwintering birds. Some wetland plants produce as much as 900 pounds of seeds per acre.[6] Birds consume not only the seeds but all parts of grasses, sedges, and rushes including tubers (modified roots), **rhizomes** (modified stems), stems, foliage, and inflorescences (flowers).

## Floating-Leaved Plants

Just as the words suggest, these plants have leaves floating on the surface of the water. They are rooted in a lake bottom and occupy those lakes that do not dry out. Water lilies (*Nymphaea spp.*) are one example that, like many floating-leaved plants, tend to form large colonies from spreading underground rhizomes (Figure 1.4). Rhizomes are modified stems that spread horizontally underground. They are often referred to informally as creeping roots, but although they resemble roots, rhizomes are really underground stems. Some floating-leaved plants can exist completely underwater for days or even months.

Floating-leaved plants live simultaneously in two habitats: water on the bottom and air on the top. A thick, waxy substance protects the leaves from the air. Wind and waves can be a problem to these plants so they typically grow in sheltered areas.

## Emergent Plants

**Emergent plants** are rooted in sediment, but the tops of the plants extend into the air. These plants grow in soils that are periodically inundated with water or are submersed. This is an ideal situation for most plants: Nutrients are available from the sediments, and water is abundantly available from the sediment and overlying water, yet carbon dioxide and sunlight are accessible from the air. The erect, narrow-leaved sedges and rushes are in this group. Grasses, sedges, and rushes are critical to the diet of many waterfowl such as ducks and geese. These plants are not restricted to the diets of birds alone; deer, rabbits, moose, cattle, alligators, beavers, and boar all consume these wetland plants.

The emergent plants face the challenge of being able to sustain the force of even subtly moving water. These plants must have strong root systems and much energy is put into creating this strong structure.

## Submersed Plants

**Submersed plants** are completely underwater. Mosses (*Fontinalis spp.*) are submersed plants that face the difficulty of obtaining light for photosynthesis. Most plants get carbon dioxide from the air where it is relatively plentiful; submersed species must get carbon dioxide from the water where it is less readily available. One of the benefits of being fully submersed is that these plants do not need to put as much energy into creating support tissue.

## Free-Floating Plants

**Free-floating plants** float at or just below the water's surface with roots that do not extend into the sediment below. These plants must obtain all of the nutrients they need from the water. Wind and waves tend to relocate them so they often end up in bays.

# 2 The Natural World of Aquatic and Wetland Plants

•  •  •  •  •  •  •  •  •  •  •  •  •  •  •  •  •  •  •  •  •  •

The aquatic world varies widely, but all aquatic and wetland plants have similar factors that regulate their growth: light availability, nutrients and water chemistry, substrate (the foundation to which an organism is attached), and wind energy. Other factors such as the shape and depth of the aquatic habitat contribute to a plant's growth.

## LIGHT

All plants need light to photosynthesize. The deeper the water, the less likely a plant will be able to receive the light it needs. Light is the limiting factor in determining the depth at which water plants will grow. A heavy sediment load as the result of runoff or erosion can reduce the amount of light that reaches below the water surface, which is why sediments are a concern in aquatic environments. The more sediment-filled a lake or pond is, the less aquatic life will be in it even if the water is relatively shallow.

Other influences of water clarity are phytoplankton and organic particles; the lower each of these are, the more clear the water is. As water clarity decreases, plant life is reduced and the littoral zone decreases. Boats, shoreline or riverbank erosion, and burrowing animals such as carp can increase suspended sediment.

## NUTRIENTS AND WATER CHEMISTRY

Plants have nutrient needs, both mineral and nonmineral. In an ecosystem, these nutrients are recycled throughout the system. The nonmineral nutrients are hydrogen (H), oxygen (O), and carbon (C). Nonmineral nutrients are found in the air and water, while mineral nutrients are found in the soil.

Nutrients that plants need in large quantities are referred to as **macronutrients**, and those they need in small amounts are called **micronutrients**. Plants need the following macronutrients: nitrogen (N), phosphorus (P), and potassium (K). Most rooted aquatic plants get phosphorus and potassium from sediments since the open seas have relatively low concentrations of these elements. For aquatic plants, limited nutrients, particularly nitrogen and phosphorus, will limit how much the plant will grow.

Aquatic and wetland plants need smaller amounts of secondary nutrients: calcium (Ca), magnesium (Mg), and sulfur (S). In even smaller quantities they need micronutrients: iron (Fe), manganese (Mn), zinc (Zn), borine (B), copper (Cu), and molybdenum (Mo). These nutrients are found in the sediments of aquatic environments.

Aquatic and wetland plants get their nutrients differently depending on how they grow. Rooted emergent plants get their nutrients from sediments. Emergent floating plants get their nutrients from the water. Submersed rooted plants get their nutrients from the sediments that the roots are in, as well as through the **water column**. The water column is the "cylinder" of water from the surface of the water body to the bottom. A creature floating on the water surface or burrowing in the sediment is not in the water column. Submersed floating plants only get their nutrients from the water column.

Nutrients and aquatic environments are in a delicate balance. Nutrient-rich lakes are more productive than nutrient-poor ones. Productivity is measured by the amount of biotic life. Too many

## Nutrient-Rich Waters: Too Much of a Good Thing?

We have all heard the expression "everything in moderation." The same is often true in nature. When an overabundance of nutrients is present in water bodies, algae and aquatic weeds will grow to the point that they will compete for oxygen and space in the water. Oxygen is an important component in all bodies of water for biotic communities. Biotic communities consist of all of the living organisms in a specified area. All these organisms have a demand for oxygen.

Fertilizers from farms and lawns can contribute to these nutrient-rich waters. This is known as eutrophication. Fertilizers are high in nutrients, and although they are valuable when the appropriate amounts are applied to desirable vegetation or crops, fertilizers in water are pollutants. Failing septic tanks can also create eutrophication because the waste products are high in organic matter. The more polluted a section of water, the more microorganisms and aquatic life compete for the oxygen in the water. High levels of pollution, even in the form of nutrients can cause fish to suffocate from lack of oxygen. Other man-made activities that lead to eutrophication are factory effluents, domestic waste discharges, feed lot runoff, and construction site erosion. Dead fish floating on the top of a body of water are one sign of nutrient-rich waters.

Many state agencies monitor surface waters for an over-abundance of nutrients. In New Jersey, the Department of Environmental Protection (DEP) requires that anyone who discharges matter into a water supply must get a permit. Procedures that will minimize an adverse impact to the water supply are required of activities that result in a discharge of nutrients. Businesses or individuals that fail to comply can be fined.

## What Are Point and Nonpoint Source Pollution?

Point source pollution consists of chemicals that enter directly into a body of water. A pipe pouring wastewater directly into a stream is point source pollution. Nonpoint source pollution is when pollutants reach a body of water after passing through or over another medium. The runoff that goes into a creek from a driveway with puddles of antifreeze and oil would be nonpoint source pollution. A malfunctioning septic system would be nonpoint source pollution. Water pollutants include any chemical or substance that degrades the quality of water for drinking. Salt and other deicers that get thrown on the road and sidewalks during the winter are sources of nonpoint source pollution. Obvious pollutants are pesticides, fertilizers, oil, and grease, but even sediment is considered a pollutant. Changes in the pattern of water flow can occur from engineering projects such as reservoirs and stream channelization. Changing the natural flow of a body of water increases sediment deposits, which in turn adversely affects aquatic life. Sediments are soil particles, and they may carry chemical pollutants and nutrients with them into the water. The suspended soil particles in the water may reduce light needed for photosynthesis by plant life and clog the gills of fish.

nutrients can also be devastating to an aquatic ecosystem because these environments have little dissolved oxygen. Nutrients in a lake are the result of management practices, watershed influences, and direct human-caused nutrient additions, such as fertilizer runoff.

Ponds tend to be more nutrient rich than rivers, and therefore ponds support a greater diversity of aquatic life. The reason is that ponds move more slowly, although biological diversity of aquatic life is a reflection of water depth, sediment type, and geology.

Just as terrestrial plants are affected by the pH of their soils, aquatic species composition is determined in part by water pH and water quality. Pollution can reduce the quality of water and therefore plant life. Neutral or alkaline water generally supports the best plant growth in ponds; shallow depth will allow in light. High concentrations of soluble iron can limit the availability of phosphorus. Excessive organic matter often contains high levels of organic acids that are toxic to aquatic vegetation. Aquatic vegetation attempts to temper these toxins by releasing oxygen from its roots. This eliminates the condition where a lack of oxygen creates toxic substances.

Common cattail (*Typha latifolia*) is a wetland plant capable of producing oxygen by its roots to counteract the difficulties of growing in an anaerobic environment. With this knowledge, scientists are able to choose plants like cattail to grow in a polluted wetland where most plants would have difficulty thriving.

## OXYGEN

Terrestrial plants exchange gases that they need, such as carbon dioxide and oxygen, through openings in the leaves known as **stomates**. Underwater leaves don't have stomates, so they must rely on intracellular spaces called **aerenchyma** that supply oxygen to the plant (Figure 2.1). The oxygen then diffuses to the lower parts of the plant.

## INVASIVE SPECIES AND COMPETITION

**Invasive species** include animals, plants, and microbes that infiltrate and invade ecosystems beyond their historic range. Their invasion threatens native ecosystems or commercial, agricultural, or recreational activities dependent on these ecosystems. They may even harm the health of humans. In some cases the native species is completely displaced. Invasive species are generally not native; they are usually from another country or region. Other terms used to describe invasive species are invaders, nonnatives, exotics, invasives, and nuisance species. These terms will be used interchangeably.

Organisms in a new environment are not a new problem. Humans traveling across the Atlantic Ocean have assisted with this invasion for centuries. Many of these invasives entered the United States back in the 1800s. In some cases they were purposefully introduced because benefit was perceived in their introduction, such as being easy to grow or having a pretty flower.

This travel transformed the existing plant and animal species. A hundred years ago people did not realize the kind

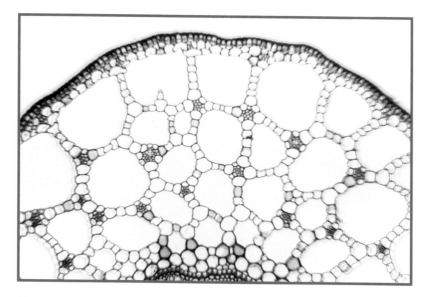

**Figure 2.1** Terrestrial plants have stomates to exchange needed gases. Stomates are openings in the leaves. Leaves that are underwater have aerenchyma instead of stomates. This photograph depicts the air passages found in the tissue of aquatic plants that enable plant roots to grow underwater.

of ecological warfare these organisms would wage on native organisms. Scientists have compared the movement of these exotic plants, animals, and microbes to a game of biological roulette. Once in a new environment, the organism might die or it might take hold and became an ecological bully by stealing nourishment and habitat from native species.

Today we see the dwindling of native species caused by these invaders. Introductions are accelerating due to travel, trade, and tourism. Whereas oceans and unscalable mountains kept animals from entering terrain where they did not belong, trade and travel have bridged any geographic barrier. A plane can take you from Philadelphia to sub-Saharan Africa. If an animal finds its way into the cargo area of a plane, it could travel thousands of miles within a day. The barriers that nature has instituted can be overcome in a day.

Invasive species are a problem because they are outstanding competitors. All creatures evolve toward becoming a better competitor. Changes occur based on the requirements of their environment. On a large scale, this drama unfolds, like much of human history, as a succession of dynasties. Organisms possessing common ancestry rise to dominance, expand their geographic ranges, and split into multiple species.[7] Some species, such as the rose, modify leaves into thorns, while another plant species might develop fruit only at the top of its canopy, out of reach of a nonclimbing predator. Those species that do not adapt and change retreat into obscurity; their populations become smaller, more compromised, and eventually extinct. All biological creatures have an innate desire to perpetuate their species. As such, clever competition is crucial.

## Clever Competition

Environments are ever-changing. Even a desert can have a day of freezing rain. And how is a plant to cope? Purple loosestrife

(*Lythrum salicaria*) possesses the ability to make physical changes in response to its immediate environment (Figure 2.2). This is not necessarily a permanent, genetic variation like mutation or adaptation but a temporary change during the life cycle of the individual plant. Changes usually consist of variation in the type and placement of new organs. One type of structural change is to elongate leaf shape to adjust to decreased levels of light.

**Phenotypic plasticity** is the term describing this variation between individual plants of the same species but growing in different environments. Think of "plastic" as something that is changeable; phenotype is the physical attributes of an organism. Some scientists prefer to think of phenotypic plasticity as plants expressing behavior. The mayapple (*Podophyllum peltatum*), a herbaceous perennial growing in rich woods, is described by scientists as "deciding" whether a particular node will develop a vegetative or sexual shoot two years before the shoot appears aboveground.[8] The plant develops a vegetative or sexual shoot based on available resources. Many scientists avoid the use of the word "decide" when referring to plants since these organisms are not conscious. However, it is important to note that plants have the capability to use internal states and external cues to be more competitive in their environment.

Considering the obvious advantages of phenotypic plasticity, it is no surprise that invasive plants use this trait in their repertoire of adapting to small variations in the environment or microenvironments. Purple loosestrife develops aerenchyma as additional parts of the plant are submerged in water. As mentioned, aerenchyma are intracellular spaces between underwater stems and leaves that supply oxygen to the plant. The oxygen then diffuses to the lower parts of the plant.

There are limits to the benefits of phenotypic plasticity. Variations could result in a switch in competitive advantage and

**Figure 2.2**  Purple loosestrife is a perennial that has aggressively invaded East Coast wetlands. This invasive plant readily adapts to its environment, making it highly competitive and able to displace native plants.

a zonation of species with different growth forms along gradients of water depth in lakes.[9] As mentioned, emergent species live in the shallow water in lakes, known as the littoral zone. Emergent species respond to their environment, specifically the water level, by growing longer stems or other support structures. Emergent species generally outcompete floating and submerged species. As the water in a lake or pond gets deeper however, the emergent species must produce much support tissue. Eventually floating-leaved species such as water lilies get the competitive edge because they are supported by buoyancy; they are not forced to grow more structures as water depth fluctuates. This is not the end of the story however. If the water depth increases further, the petioles (leaf stalks) that tether a lily's leaves to its roots must also get longer, and this occurs at the expense of allocation of leaves. Floating-leaved species such as these are then replaced by submerged species with short petioles.[10]

Another way to compete is by vigorous vegetative propagation. Growing from cut pieces of root is one method of propagating vegetatively. Many aquatic and wetland weeds are adapted to fragment easily so that they can be dispersed.

## Plant Adaptations

Adaptations enable plants to compete more effectively. **Adaptations** are changes in the species that cause a genetic variation and increase an organism's ability to survive. One of the most remarkable adaptations in the aquatic plant world is the carnivorous behavior of the bladderwort (*Utricularia sp.*). Tiny traps or bladders on the leaves catch very small organisms such as paramecia. This adaptation allows the bladderwort to get nutrients from the paramecia that it would not be able to get from the water.

Salt water is corrosive to most plants. Plants in these marine environments must find ways to resist the corrosive nature of salt.

## Reduced to Ash: The Threatened Mangroves

The Black River meanders through the southern coast of Jamaica, matching the relaxed pace of the residents. Adjacent to the river are thatch palms and majestic mangroves with tentacle-like roots rising in grandeur and resembling pipe organs. An American crocodile peeks its head out of the slow-moving water and barely notices the tourists in the small boat on the river. River safari trips traverse 6 miles (9.5 kilometers) in this region of Jamaica that sees much fewer tourists than the coastal towns. While tourists snorkel in the coral reefs of northern Jamaica, the ecological treasure of the mangroves is diminishing. Mangroves are a haven for fish and other wildlife; they protect the shoreline and purify the water by removing pollutants. Their sturdy roots that enable them to withstand constant contact with water are also the source of their demise.

In Jamaica, mangroves are disappearing because their value is little recognized and conservation efforts are relatively recent. Mangroves make an excellent source of wood and charcoal in a country where fire is the only source of fuel for many people. The destruction of the mangroves threatens the fishing industry that the people also rely on. Conservation efforts to preserve the remaining mangroves have focused on educating Jamaicans about the importance of these ecosystems.

In tropical locations in Florida, Panama, Australia, and Bermuda, turtle grass *(Thalassia testudinum)* is a sea grass that masters the adaptation of resistance to salt water in the shallow, sandy areas just off shore. Only the adult straplike leaves can resist the corrosive nature of salt. Turtle grass protects the young leaves by growing a protective, cushiony sheath over them. Pushing on the sheath shows the resilience of this package and the water that is contained within it. The water contained within the sheath is not the salt water that the grass is in but freshwater that the plant has desalinated. When the leaf has matured enough to develop a resistance to salt water, it grows out of the protective sheath and another shoot is left behind.

Mangroves are another type of plant living in salt water that must deal with the problem of salt in the environment (Figure 2.3). Mangroves are woody plants living in **brackish** waters of tropical and subtropical regions between the sea and land in areas inundated by tides. Brackish waters are where freshwater and salt water mix.

Mangroves provide a habitat for fish and protect shores from harsh waves. Without salt-excreting mechanisms, the roots

**Figure 2.3**  Mangroves are well known for their tentacle-like roots. Mangroves are a vital part of the aquatic ecosystem, serving as a haven for fish and protecting the shoreline from harsh waves. In many countries, mangroves are being lost because of their value as firewood. Pictured above is a black mangrove swamp in Texas.

would rot from being submerged in salt water. Salt that enters the system is quickly excreted by salt glands on the leaves. These glands are some of the most effective salt-excreting systems known in the natural world, and a lick of the mangrove leaves will show how salty they can get. Mangroves also filter out the salt at the root level. A third method that mangroves use to get rid of salt is to concentrate it in the bark or older leaves that will soon fall from the plant.

Another clever adaptation of the mangrove is having its roots above water to get oxygen. Little oxygen is available in fine, often waterlogged mud. Roots grow upward above the mud, giving them access to oxygen yet keeping the plant properly supported. Lenticels, or special breathing cells, cover the roots and draw in air. The number of lenticels changes along the root structure as more oxygen is available. More oxygen availability means more lenticels, and vice versa.

## HOW PLANTS REPRODUCE

Plants reproduce by seeds, spores, or vegetative parts. Plants that live for one growing season, called annuals, generally produce large numbers of seeds. Biennials are plants that complete their life cycle in two growing seasons and reproduce by both seeds and roots. Perennials live for more than two growing seasons, with some long-lived herbaceous perennials living decades, such as Canada thistle (*Cirsium arvense*). Perennials generally focus energy into significant root growth, although there are exceptions such as purple loosestrife, which is a prolific seed-producing perennial.

### Vegetative Reproduction

Root segments or pieces that contain a node can reproduce to form a new plant. Root segments are cut by farming equipment, boat propellers, gardening tools, and any other tool that is used where plants exist and can segment a root.

Waterfowl consume all aquatic and wetland plant parts. Shoots or suckers are consumed, pass through migratory waterfowl, and are spread to new sites. People dumping the water in home aquariums into streams, creeks, ponds, and lakes are also another source of invasive plant introductions. Boats moving from one body of water to another also spread invasive aquatic plants. The propellers are perfect for entangling plants. When boaters dock, very few take the time to clean their boats. Many state natural resource agencies are educating boaters about how to properly clean their boats to prevent spreading invasive aquatic plants.

**Figure 2.4** Flowering plants, or angiosperms, produce seeds to reproduce sexually. The daisy *(left)* is one of many thousands of species of flowering plants. Ferns *(right)* are gymnosperms. Gymnosperms do not flower; they produce spores to reproduce sexually.

## Sexual Reproduction

All flowering plants, or **angiosperms,** produce seeds. Not all plants are flowering, however; some plants produce spores for reproduction and these plants are classified as **gymnosperms** (Figure 2.4). Pine trees are one example of a plant that bears spores in cones.

Aquatic plants have unique ways of reproducing to ensure the perpetuation of their species. Coontail (*Ceratophyllum demersum*) has developed structures referred to as winter buds. The winter bud is a dense mass of foliage produced on the top portion of the plant that contains an embryo plant. This bud is also packed with food reserves for the embryo plant since it will need these reserves for early growth. As the winter bud develops in the fall, it detaches from the parent plant and sinks to the bottom. In spring, it will form a new plant. Other aquatic plants disperse pollen over the water's surface where some may arrive on the stigma of a plant.

# What Makes Some Aquatic and Wetland Plants Invasive?

**3**

One of the dangers of invasive aquatic and wetland plants is that their populations increase exponentially each year without any constraints, which alters fragile ecosystems. Wetlands can become so clogged by the overgrowth of invasive plant species that native birds will no longer make the wetland their home.

Invasive plant species threaten the supply of freshwater. Aquatic invasive species (all species, not just plants) continue to arrive in the Great Lakes at a rate of one every eight months, adding to the more than 160 species already causing serious ecological and economic damage. One of the most notorious invasive species in the Great Lakes is the zebra mussel (*Dreissena polymorpha*). The zebra mussel is a 1-inch-long (2.5 centimeters) exotic mollusk that has devastated native mussels in the Great Lakes. Each invasive species has the potential to have disastrous results on aquatic systems.

## AWAY FROM HOME WITHOUT THEIR NATURAL ENEMIES

In their native countries, invasive aquatic and wetland species are kept in control by natural predators. As these invaders found their way into other environments, the organisms that keep their populations in control were left behind. Natural predators include fish or plant pathogens (diseases) that are crucial to nature's natural balance of predator and prey (Figure 3.1).

Predator-prey relationships are the interactions where one species is a food source or prey for the other species. A predator is the animal that eats the other. Prey is the animal that the predator is eating. Predators and prey in action have been depicted on nature shows on television, for instance, where the cheetah outruns and eats the gazelle. Although not quite as dramatic, insects and plants have predator-prey relationships as well.

Predators and prey evolve together and occur naturally in the environment. The predator encourages the fittest of the prey species. The prey will try to avoid being eaten and will therefore develop characteristics to prevent death. The prey may evolve to be faster if the predator is a chasing animal. The prey may also develop a better sense of smell, sight, or camouflage. Characteristics that the prey possesses that do not enable it to escape the predator would not be improved or refined. Similarly, characteristics of predators that enable them to catch their prey, like claws, sharp teeth, and keen eyesight, would be developed over time.

Predator-prey relationships are nature's way of keeping species in balance. The predator's population may be larger than usual one season but will decrease in a later one because of the limits on food (the prey). Separating the predator from its prey knocks the system out of balance and causes a potentially damaging situation for the environment—a "superspecies" may emerge for which there are few controls on the population.

## GETTING AROUND THE GLOBE

Plants have their own form of travel. If they didn't, plant species would be localized to one small section of the Earth. Possessing the ability to be transported around the globe presents the possibility of ending up in places never intended by nature.

**Figure 3.1**   The predator-prey relationship keeps populations in control. Invasive species lack predators, and this enables them to keep expanding their populations. In this photograph, an insect (prey) rests on the jaw-like leaf of a Venus flytrap (predator).

## Floods: Friend or Foe of Invasive Plants?

Flooding can cause a new invasive aquatic or wetland plant invasion but it can also be used to control invasives. Flooding is a type of disturbance, just as plowing, fire, or any other practice that disrupts the soil profile and denudes the surface of vegetation. Invasive plant species love disturbance because it provides an opportunity of establishment.

Flooding is a natural function of a river system. Spring flooding introduces nutrients into the soil surrounding the root system of riverbank trees, such as cottonwoods. Human influences, however, have altered natural systems, and flooding occurs on an unnatural timetable in many places. Flooding, however, clearly affords the opportunity for invasive plant species to become easily established. In addition, the seeds of many invasive aquatic and wetland plants float, and flooding can help disperse seeds great distances. If the force of the flood is truly strong enough, fragmented roots of biennials and perennials can also be sent miles downstream.

Flooding has also been used to a limited extent to control aquatic and wetland invasive plants. In water bodies where the level can be regulated, weeds can be submerged. Scientists submerged 4-week-old saltcedar seedlings for 30 days and found a 98% mortality rate.* Unfortunately, flooding cannot be used selectively, so if other desirable species are present, they are likely to die or be injured, as well.

*Matthew Sprenger and L.M. Smith "Testing Control of Saltcedar Seedlings Using Fall Flooding." *Wetlands* 21, no. 3 (2001): p. 437.

## Sea Ballast Water

A ship leaves a port in the Indian Ocean with a cargo of rice and travels through the Suez Canal. The ship unloads the rice at a port in the Mediterranean and must take up millions of gallons of water to maintain its weight and therefore stability in transport. The ship then crosses the Atlantic Ocean and enters the Great Lakes to pick up wheat for transport to a receiving port. The water that the ship took up to maintain stability, referred to as **ballast water**, is no longer needed when cargo is put on the ship. This ballast water is dumped in the Great Lakes, where nonnative organisms are introduced into a foreign environment. Species that are native to one port are suddenly the outsiders in another port thousands of miles away. Scientists estimate that as many as 3,000 alien species per day are transported in ships around the world. These organisms range from microscopic plants and animals to crabs, mussels, and even schools of fish. Not all of these species survive, but some are able to thrive as "bioinvaders." These exotic species are often transported without their natural predators and their populations can grow out of control. Some of these nonnatives can even cause human disease. *Vibrio cholerae* is a bacterium that causes a severe diarrheal disease called Asiatic cholera or epidemic cholera. This bacterium is one of the most common organisms in surface waters. It was introduced to Asia likely through shipping. Scientists have isolated this organism in ballast water of cargo ships from the Gulf of Mexico. Cholera has been referred to in literature dating back to Ancient Greece, and has been associated with numerous epidemics after being introduced into a new location.

No single management technique has proven successful in killing or removing all organisms in ballast water. Selecting a treatment method depends on the structural integrity of the ship and its size, the expense of method, amount of potential damage to the environment, safety of the crew, and ease for port authorities to monitor compliance.

One option is open sea exchange. In the above example, instead of the ship discharging in the Great Lakes, it would empty the ballast water in the open sea, the Atlantic Ocean in this case, and then fill the ballast tank with ocean water. This method works because coastal organisms are unlikely to be able to survive in the open sea. The option has the appeal of being easily monitored since a simple salinity test would be able to detect whether the ballast water is seawater or freshwater. Open sea exchange is not safe, however, when the seas are stormy or rough. Another limitation is that sediments and residual water are difficult to remove from the ballast tank.

Biocides can also be used to treat ballast water by killing organisms. One concern is for the health of the crew handling these chemicals. Another concern is the potential of corroding the ballast tank. Ballast water can also be heated to temperatures between 95°F to 113°F (35°C to 45°C) to kill larger organisms such as fish, but this will not kill all microorganisms. No easy solution to this major pathway of biological invasions exists. Until recently, treating ballast water wasn't given a high priority. Research continues for techniques to treat ballast water without jeopardizing the safety of crew members.

## Hull Fouling

Sea ballast water accidentally carries organisms inside the ship, whereas hull fouling carries organisms outside the ship where they attach to the hull. Organisms such as barnacles, mussels, sea squirts, sponges, and algae are able to attach to the hull and be transported long distances. Once they arrive in a new port, they can create new exotic populations by releasing their larvae (immature offspring) or attaching to another structure in the port. Hull fouling can easily be solved by building metal hulls and applying antifouling paints to prevent organisms from attaching to the hull. As shipping increases, it becomes vitally important to incorporate these preventative measures to prevent an exotic species explosion.

## THE EFFECTS ON NATIVE ORGANISMS

Native organisms have evolved with natural predators and disease. Predators and disease control their populations. The unfair advantage that nonnative plants have is usually too great for native populations. Without intervention to remove nonnative invasive plants, native plants will generally become displaced, eventually to the point of complete exclusion. In aquatic and wetland communities, organisms that rely on native plants will be adversely affected. Fish will no longer have a food source; birds will have to go elsewhere for nesting sites, and often, the invasive plant grows so thickly that animals cannot physically access or navigate the water.

Invasive aquatic and wetland plants compete for sunlight, nutrients, and water. Generally, they are more aggressive than their native counterparts at acquiring these resources and taking the available resources, leaving little for native plants. The result is a shift from a biologically diverse plant community to a monoculture of one invasive species.

## CLOGGING WATERWAYS

Invasive species are notorious for rapid growth. Not only does this rapid growth suck up large amounts of resources, including water, the undesirable vegetation inhibits waterways. Turbines, dams, canals, and ditches become choked with weeds; removal is often costly. Without consistent removal, waterways would be brought to a standstill and their function would be rendered useless.

## Link It Up or Break It Up?

When it comes to habitat preservation, linking natural areas is best. If you had a total of ten acres to preserve, it would be best to have ten acres all in the same location, not ten one-acre parcels. Creating small parcels of protected areas is the ecological equivalent to creating islands where species are more isolated than those living on a vast land mass.

Species on an island or isolated parcel don't have access to other populations; therefore they would not be able to mate with one another. Geographic isolation reduces gene flow between populations, and the resulting gene pool is isolated, less diverse, and smaller. With animals, as a gene pool becomes more and more narrow, inbreeding will occur, which reduces genetic diversity and weakens the species. Colonization is when species occupy a region that was previously not part of their range. Colonization increases biological diversity, assuming the new species is not an invasive plant, animal, or microbe. When populations are diverse and natural systems are functioning properly, species will become more fit, change over time, or evolve.

Preserved land that is larger in size generally has greater species diversity and gene flow between populations. Most important, new plant or animal populations will become genetically divergent from their parent population due to natural selection and mutation.

Habitat fragmentation adversely affects animal and plant populations. Once a habitat has been fragmented, there is not much that can be done to restore a species. Because of this, preserving land should focus more on creating corridors rather than islands of preservation.

# Invasive Wetland Plants  4

· · · · · · · · · · · · · · · · · · · · · · · · · · · · · · · · · · · · · · · · · · · · · ·

Wetlands are highly productive systems. The availability of water enables the system to maintain this high level of productivity by providing food and shelter for a variety of organisms. As with any ecosystem, interaction among species and recycling of nutrients within the system is critical. An aggressive outsider, such as purple loosestrife, giant reed, reed canarygrass, or giant hogweed, just to name a few, can interrupt these interactions to the extent that the wetland is not performing to its potential any longer.

## INVASIVE WETLAND GRASSES

At Joppa Flats just outside of Boston, dunes and barrier beaches, salt marshes, and a red maple swamp sprawl out on protected acres within sight of boats on the Atlantic Ocean. Tall stands of cordgrass and saltmeadow grass sway in the gentle breeze as herons and egrets dip below the water's surface to find food. The distinctive "will-will-willet-willet-willet" is heard as a willet passes overhead displaying strong white wingbars. Butterflies extract nectar from purple coneflower (*Echinacea ssp.*), and though not visible, the larvae of the pearl crescent butterfly finds refuge in an aster. Behind the Joppa Flats Education Center, Gerome, their resident green heron, has again taken up its roost in the restored marsh behind the building.

It is only recently that many of the native birds and insects have returned to this breathtaking protected area. Joppa Flats is managed by the Massachusetts Audubon Society and the U.S. Fish and Wildlife Agency. Staff members identify and dig out invasive plants that threaten these wetland ecosystems.

Phragmites (*Phragmites communis*), also called common reed, threatened to evict native birds until the staff tackled the tedious chore of pulling it out by hand. Phragmites' country of origin is unclear. It may actually be from the United States. Scientists have been able to find evidence that phragmites has been present in North American wetlands for 3,000 years, yet this plant has definitely been invading wetlands much more aggressively in recent years. Some scientists believe that the increased spread is due to phragmites' breeding with similar European wetland plants, creating a hardier hybrid. Others believe that the increase in phragmites might be attributed to changes in water quality, where pollution has caused water that is more nutrient rich. Nutrient-rich waters are problematic because they have less oxygen available for aquatic life.

Although phragmites may be native, it is still considered an invasive plant. It spreads quickly by underground stems or rhizomes. Reaching nearly 10 feet (3 meters) in height, this invasive provides little value to wildlife. In addition, its dense growth inhibits light from reaching the ground and therefore prevents other plants from growing. Although phragmites is still present, manageable levels prevent the devastating effects of complete native vegetation loss.

The plants in these wetlands provide a source of food and habitat for fish. Many birds then rely on the fish for food. Native vegetation is used for nesting.

As all insects do, butterflies require a home during the larval state. Plants like milkweed are an important larval refuge, particularly for the brilliantly colored orange and black monarch butterfly.

## Invasion of the Clones: Giant Reed

Out of the low, scrubby vegetation in coastal California, a sequence of sharp, slurred phrases ending with an ascending note can be heard as a hiker passes through the brush. The hiker takes out a pair of binoculars and spots a bird with whitish cheeks and greenish wings and tail. The hiker, who also happens to be an experienced birder, recognizes the bird she has previously only seen in pictures: the federally endangered least Bell's vireo. Once widespread, the least Bell's vireo has become endangered because of loss and degradation of stream and river corridors through development, flood control projects, agriculture, and

**Figure 4.1**  Giant reed, native to India, is invading freshwater habitats from California to Maryland. Although the giant reed's seeds are sterile, it can reproduce rapidly through rhizomes.

invasive species. Giant reed is responsible for degrading the habitat that this bird species relies on.

Giant reed (*Arundo donax*) produces sterile seeds yet is so aggressive in its vegetative reproduction that it has become a nuisance in freshwater habitats from California to Maryland (Figure 4.1). Capable of reaching 30 feet (9 meters) in height, this grass is native to India. Giant reed was introduced to North America in the early 1800s for erosion control, as an ornamental, as windbreak, to thatch roofs, and to make clarinet and bassoon reeds.

Giant reed is a perennial with rhizomes that grow or "creep" underground and emerge aboveground as a new plant. Fragmented stem or root pieces can also form new plants. Plants that are formed vegetatively are genetically identical, essentially clones. Giant reed can form huge clones covering hundreds of acres. This invasive plant does not provide food or habitat for native wildlife and is considered one of the greatest threats to native riparian, or riverbank, habitats in the Southwest.

Efforts to control giant reed should be focused on the populations farthest upstream since the fragmented roots tend to float downstream. The extensive system of rhizomes makes success by handpulling alone seem unlikely, although anything is possible with enough diligence and a limited area to bring under control. Aquatic herbicides have proven effective, although repeated treatments and monitoring are always recommended.

## A Green Carpet: Reed Canarygrass

Since they were just barely old enough to ride their bikes, John and Matt would ride to Otter Creek Marsh to look at the tadpoles and waterbugs in the shallow areas. They looked forward to the day they could bring their poles, fish by themselves, and catch something to show off to their parents. Each year the water seemed to get more and more murky. The boys didn't know it, but the marsh was filling with silt.

**Siltation** is the process by which a waterway accumulates greater amounts of silt. Some causes of siltation are cropping and grazing, runoff, and construction, essentially any activity that causes soil to erode and run off into the waterway. The boys only know that they can no longer see the tadpoles. They grab a stick and swish it in the water to see if there is any movement. Nothing. This is one effect of siltation—a decrease in aquatic life. Siltation causes a decrease in water clarity, which then causes a decrease in plant life because light can't get through the water. With plant life decreased, the fish that depend on plants are compromised. The cause of siltation at Otter Creek Marsh is reed canarygrass (*Phalaris arundinacea*).

Reed canarygrass is a perennial grass that spreads via rhizomes and frequently occupies areas along rivers (Figure 4.2). It may grow so densely that water flow is slowed. Slower water is less able to carry sediment, and therefore it is deposited, causing

**Figure 4.2**    The dense growth of reed canarygrass slows the flow of water. As shown, reed canarygrass can be so aggressive that it outcompetes all other native vegetation.

the siltation. This weed can grow in saturated or nearly saturated soils but not where standing water persists for long periods.

This invasive plant, spread by seeds and rhizomes, has become a significant threat to wetlands because of its ability to completely dominate an ecosystem to the exclusion of native plants. Whereas native vegetation provides habitat and food for native wildlife, reed canarygrass provides little value. Few species will eat the grass and it grows too densely to provide adequate cover for waterfowl and mammals. In addition, the abundant pollen that the grass produces is the source of hay fever and allergies for many people.

Despite the ill effects of this invasive plant, reed canarygrass is planted as a forage crop and is an important component of lowland hay in the Midwest. The obvious first step in control is to prevent it from being cultivated as animal feed. Once it has become established, herbicides can be used but must be safe for use in aquatic areas. Burning has also been successful when it is combined with reseeding or herbicides. Mechanical removal using heavy equipment does not work well because the plants readily resprout and the soil disturbance encourages seeds to germinate. Mowing twice a year to prevent seed production has had some success, assuming that some native plants still exist. Attempts to control this weed have even involved cutting it down to the ground level and covering it with opaque, black plastic tarps. Without a source of sunlight, the weeds underneath the tarp should, in theory, starve. Reed canarygrass, though, has been able to push up through almost any material.

## INVASIVE EMERSED PLANTS

Along the Delaware Canal in Pennsylvania, a preserved historical park is a head-turning picture of purple loosestrife blooms framed by a narrow rim of cattails. Most visitors to the park are unaware of the ecological red flag of a solid stand of one species.

This formerly biologically rich community once teeming with native birds, butterflies, perennials, sedges, and rushes, now has little to offer these organisms. The longer it takes for a control plan to be implemented, the more acres of habitat are lost to invasive **emersed plants** (plants that rise above the surface of the water).

## The Scourge of the East: Purple Loosestrife

Purple loosestrife is a deep-rooted perennial with striking, brilliantly colored flowers of pink and purple. This invasive was introduced in the 1800s as an ornamental from Eurasia (the continent where Asia and Europe are located) and is taking over millions of wetland areas and displacing native plants.

Purple loosestrife reproduces by seeds and roots. Although annuals are usually credited with being prolific seed producers, purple loosestrife has remarkable production of seeds per plant. Scientists from the United States Geological Survey found the average number of seeds per plant to be 2,700,000.[11] Not all seeds float, but purple loosestrife seeds do and this is a significant method of dispersal. This is quite helpful to purple loosestrife's efforts to spread considering the wet locations it generally occupies.

Purple loosestrife seeds are small and are spread by wind to a limited extent. The low mass and small size of purple loosestrife seeds make them likely to be spread in mud adhering to aquatic wildlife, livestock, the tread of all-terrain vehicles, boots of hunters, or on the hulls of barges.[12] Longer-range distributions of purple loosestrife are accomplished by seeds caught in the plumage of migratory birds.

Purple loosestrife spreads vegetatively by adventitious shoots and roots often from cut stems. Adventitious roots occur in

## Genetically Engineering Sterile Plants: Method of Control or Just a Misconception?

Many invasive plants are beautiful. Purple loosestrife found its way to the United States because of its eye-catching blossoms. Convincing people that they should pull such a benign-looking plant is often met with resistance. Even those who consider themselves ecologically minded will often defend the weed with a shrug and an offhand remark such as "but it's pretty." Such attitudes prove a challenge to natural resource managers trying to convince landowners to remove these invasive plants from their own properties.

Another challenge to controlling plants like purple loosestrife is the availability of sterile varieties of invasive plants. Sterile varieties are genetically altered to produce non-viable, or sterile, seeds. In some cases a small percentage, maybe just 1%, of the seeds are still viable. Although the majority of the seeds can't produce a new purple loosestrife plant, 1% of all seeds produced can. One purple loosestrife plant can produce more than 2 million seeds

unusual locations on a plant, such as up on a stem. The ability of purple loosestrife to survive vegetatively is aided by its ability to live in a variety of environments, both wet and dry. Plants that can live in a wide variety of environments are known as **generalist species**. Most nonnative plants that are invasive are generalists. Plants with very specific roles in an ecosystem are known as **specialist species.**

### Altering habitats

Purple loosestrife was introduced without its natural predators and is able to take the energy that would be spent fighting disease and insects and spend it on rapid growth and seed production. Purple per season. A sterile variety can therefore produce 27,000 viable seeds in one season. Most consumers are usually not aware of the high number of seeds that a sterile variety can still produce. Some sterile varieties of purple loosestrife plants do not produce a seed capsule, so no seeds are formed.

Plants can still be aggressive even if they are not able to spread by seeds. Giant reed and giant salvinia both produce sterile seeds and sporangia, yet their populations have become a nuisance in aquatic and wetland environments. Even if a sterile purple loosestrife plant was not able to produce viable seeds, it could still reproduce vegetatively.

The best alternative is to find a similar-looking plant that is either native or is at least known to "behave." Liatris *(Liatris ssp.)* is a native perennial with a purple flower that is a great alternative for people who find purple loosestrife appealing.

loosestrife is so aggressive that **monocultures,** or communities of only one species, and in this case only purple loosestrife, can be seen throughout East Coast wetlands (Figure 4.3).

Generally wetlands are more biologically diverse than other habitats because of water availability; therefore, an invasive plant has a greater opportunity to crowd out many species. In the process of displacing native plants, food and habitat are ruined for native wildlife. Native birds will not eat the seeds of purple loosestrife and ducks find wetlands infested with purple loosestrife too dense for nesting.

The bog turtle (*Clemmys muhlenbergi*) is also on the decline in purple loosestrife-infested waters. This small and uncommon reptile requires a habitat of shallow, standing water and wet, open fen or meadow. Purple loosestrife grows much too densely for the bog turtle, so dense that recreationists also have a difficult time accessing these waters.

The black tern (*Chlidonias niger*) also finds these altered wetlands unsuitable. Black terns prefer shallow ponds in the Great Plains and have suffered recent declines. Terns need bark, twigs, and other organic debris for nesting. When most of the native vegetation has been displaced by purple loosestrife, the habitat is rendered just as useless to native wildlife as if the wetland was filled with concrete.

Another frightening aspect of this invader is the seeming ability to halt the natural process of succession. As stated

**Figure 4.3** Invasive plants such as purple loosestrife can transform a diverse wetland into a monoculture. Purple loosestrife provides little food for native birds and the vegetation is too dense for nesting birds.

previously, succession is the gradual replacement of one set of plant species for another, starting with pioneer species and ending with a climax community. Purple loosestrife, in its environment of origin, is a pioneer species but as it establishes into a uniform stand, species no longer are able to replace the purple loosestrife. Self-replacing purple loosestrife stands have been reported for 20 years without any indication of species replacement. Without an aggressive management plan accompanied by restoration, the natural process of succession does not reach a climax community.

## Prevention and early detection

The good news is that purple loosestrife has not yet invaded the majority of wetlands that exist in the United States, particularly in western states. With the knowledge of how devastating this plant can be, land managers have instituted programs to react quickly to even one single purple loosestrife plant that pops up along a roadside or marsh, or is even unknowingly planted in a garden.

In Colorado, Dave Weber of the Colorado Division of Wildlife is called the Purple Loosestrife Warrior. As a wildlife biologist he knows the devastating effects of purple loosestrife on wildlife habitats. Since 1993, Weber has been working to eradicate purple loosestrife from the Denver area. Seasonal staff members map where purple loosestrife is found and then spray a herbicide during the summer before seeds are produced. Because of the extensive root system, follow-up applications must be done and the site must be monitored long term. This is an example of early detection and rapid response, which is most effective when a weed has not yet become widespread. Developing this aggressive, complete eradication approach on a known invasive plant is the most economical approach to controlling invasive species.

## Purple loosestrife management

Weeds that grow near or in water present additional obstacles to management. Contaminating the water supply with herbicides is one concern; only chemicals that can be sprayed near or in water can be used. Safe and effective herbicides do exist for the control of purple loosestrife. Most herbicides used will selectively kill all broadleaf plants along with the purple loosestrife. Land managers trying to maintain the ecological integrity of a community may lose some desirable vegetation in the process of spraying for weeds.

In addition, access usually is limited in wet and swampy areas. Using a large mower to cut weeds is much more feasible on dry, flat land. Anybody who tries to use a mower near water will only do it once because they are likely to get stuck in the mud. Handpulling or weed-whacking has limited success in controlling this plant because the deep roots will resprout unless they are all extracted. Amazingly, seeds can still form from the cut flowers of purple loosestrife. So if the weed has already flowered, all cut plants must be bagged and disposed of in a landfill or burned. This is a much more tedious process than mowing and leaving cut plants behind.

## Biological control

Introducing an insect that is a predator to control an invasive plant is a biological control technique. The danger of biological control is that it requires introducing another non-native to solve the original problem of an exotic introduction. This new species could become a pest as well and potentially more difficult to control.

Scientists recommend introducing insects that eat only the invasive plant as biological control agents. The way they test this is to quarantine the insect in a confined area and offer it a variety of plants. Scientists make sure that the insect they are introducing will eat only the invasive plant.

Some of the experiments involve withholding any plants that the insect would eat and offering a crop or other valuable plant to see if the insect will eat it if it only has a choice between eating the valuable plant or starvation. Insects are carefully monitored to see what they are eating. If the insect is willing to starve before eating the other plant, it increases its chances of being considered suitable for introduction.

In places where access is tricky, biological control is a more appealing alternative because insects can be dispersed easily and treatments do not need to be repeated yearly, although monitoring is recommended. In places where purple loosestrife monocultures have invaded a wetland many years ago, biological control may prove to be the only long-term solution.

Natural predators of purple loosestrife were found in western and central Europe where the weed grows today but is not aggressive due to these predators. There were 120 predators of purple loosestrife found, and 14 of them were considered host specific. **Host-specific** means that the predator will only attack one plant or host. Host-specificity studies were conducted for six of the species: a fly (*Dasineura salicariae*) that produces galls in plants and can reduce foliage by 75% and seed production by 80%; a stem- [and root-boring weevil (*Hylobius transversovittatus*); two beetles (*Pyrrhalta calmariensis* and *P. pusilla*) that cause nearly 50% defoliation; and two weevils (*Nanophyes marmoratuf and N. brevis*) that destroy ovaries and seeds by either eating them or using them to lay eggs.[13]

Unlike herbicides, results from introducing insects are not immediate. Populations of insects need time to build and exert a significant impact. A visible reduction in the weed varies from three to eight years but also assumes that the initial population of insects survives. Biological control release sites need to be monitored to be sure that the insects are thriving. If the initial population of insects does not survive and the monitoring is neglected, this could lead to a rapid spread of the weed that was targeted for control.

Assuming that the population does survive and grow, it will provide a terrific resource for additional biological control initiatives. Insects can be harvested from the site after a few years. Insects are collected with a sweep net and often put in a waxless ice-cream container to be transported to another weed infestation. If the distance is not too great, insects can be relocated relatively easily with little resources, primarily just labor. Even if the distance is more substantial, insects can still be relocated and are sometimes even shipped through the mail. Dry ice is used to slow their activity and minimize the risk of death from travel.

## Queen Anne's Evil Twin: Giant Hogweed

In Seattle, Washington, the King County Noxious Weed Control Board is serious about giant hogweed (*Heracleum mantegazzianum*). Informational flyers are available to hikers and naturalists warning them about this massive plant that causes painful burns on the skin (Figure 4.4). Residents who come across this introduced ornamental can report it online by filling out an infestation form. King County staff members also have specific guidelines, known as Best Management Practices in natural resources, to control this weed. Giant hogweed is listed as a noxious weed, meaning that it is restricted by law; landowners are required to remove it from their property. In addition, it is given Class A (versus B or C) status where the goal is complete eradication instead of simple management.

Giant hogweed, originally from Asia, contains a clear, toxic, watery sap that causes photodermatitis. The skin suddenly becomes hypersensitive to sunlight, resulting in painful, burning

**Figure 4.4**  Giant hogweed is an invasive plant with a toxic sap that causes painful, burning blisters. This invasive plant prefers moist soils and has therefore invaded wetlands.

blisters that may develop into purplish scars. It reaches an impressive 10 to 15 feet (3 to 4.5 meters) in height with coarse white hairs and hollow stems, and resembles Queen Anne's lace. This member of the parsley family prefers moist soils and can rapidly dominate wetlands. Giant hogweed produces winged seeds that are easily dispersed by wind, water, and soil movement.

# Invasive Floating-Leaved Plants

**5**

Invasive floating-leaved plants occupy the upper and middle littoral zone and are not rooted into the sediments. They primarily use the buoyancy of water for support.

## THE WORLD'S WORST AQUATIC WEED: GIANT SALVINIA

In Swinney Marsh, Texas, two long-time friends return to an old fishing hole to catch up on old times and snag a few fish. Coolers packed, suntan lotion applied, they plan to make a peaceful morning of fishing. They hope their favorite spot hasn't been discovered; it is the best spot for catching the bass, crappie, and sunfish notorious in Swinney Marsh. From the distance, they shield their eyes from the sun and are relieved to see no one in sight. Arriving at their spot, their poles dangle limply in their hands as they stand speechless. Neither one of them has ever seen the plant before but they both know enough about fishing to know there are no fish. Dense green mats cover the water, preventing any diversity of plant life as well as removing food for valuable fish. These dense mats are known as giant salvinia (*Salvinia molesta*) and are so thick that the men can't even cast a line into these waters. The fishermen leave, never to return to their favorite fishing hole.

Giant salvinia is one of the most aggressive aquatic weeds and is capable of overtaking all native plants in an aquatic

**Figure 5.1**  Giant salvinia is a rootless fern that can rapidly blanket a body of water. The dense cover prevents light from entering the water and therefore crowds out other aquatic vegetation.

system (Figure 5.1). The dense vegetative cover that this weed forms prevents light and atmospheric oxygen from entering the water. Decomposing plant parts consume the dissolved oxygen needed by fish and other aquatic life.

Giant salvinia is a rootless, aquatic fern. Ferns are gymnosperms, not angiosperms, meaning that they produce spores instead of seeds for reproduction. They do not flower. The submersed leaves contain elongated chains of **sporocarps**. Sporocarps are outer sacs that contain numerous sporangia, which are the equivalent of seeds in flowering plants. Mature plants produce large quantities of sporocarps but oddly enough

**Figure 5.2**   This weevil helps to control giant salvinia by damaging the plant. This insect tunnels through rhizomes and eats buds. Introducing insects to control invasive plants is a type of biological control.

are usually empty of microscopic spores or contain only a few deformed remnants.[14] Giant salvinia is considered a sterile plant because it does not produce viable spores. Despite the fact that giant salvinia is restricted to vegetative reproduction, it is taking over freshwater sources such as lakes and ponds, slow-moving rivers, canals, ditches, swamps, marshes, and rice fields at a frightening pace. Populations have been found

## Are Islands More Vulnerable?

Visitors of the Galápagos Islands, 1,500 miles west of the coast of Ecuador, must walk slowly over a foam antimicrobial mat before their passports are verified and their shoes touch Galápagos soil. It was here, on this 15-island trove of species adaptations, that Charles Darwin theorized about changes over time, or more specifically, evolution. The antimicrobial mat is an attempt to kill exotic species, perhaps a microbe or two that could foster disease and decimate a resident bird such as the blue-footed booby.

But does such ecological richness come with a heightened vulnerability to exotic species invasions and the damage they can cause? Some ecologists believe that islands are more vulnerable to invasive species because the native species haven't been evolving as much as their counterparts in continental ecosystems since there are fewer individuals to breed and interact with; essentially, the native species on an island are less fit. If species are truly less fit, they will have a more difficult time competing with invasive aquatic and wetland plants. Because island ecosystems are smaller, they are usually less biologically rich than a large ones. British ecologist Charles Elton explains in his 1958 book, *The Ecology of Invasions by Animals and Plants,* the link between *biological diversity—* the number and variety of native species in an ecosystem—and to double in size every two to four days in labs with optimal conditions.[15]

Stems fragment spontaneously as plants mature. New branches develop from buds along the top and sides. Like most invasive plants, giant salvinia is a hardy plant and will withstand periods of low temperature and dewatering through latent buds (buds that can become new plants).

ecological health. Greater diversity conveys "biotic resistance," which helps preserve the integrity of an ecosystem over time.* Other scientists argue that a smaller ecosystem simply means that there are fewer individuals and that a major event such as a hurricane may be more likely to wipe out an entire species. The Galápagos Islands have seen plenty of visitors over the centuries despite their remote location. Those seafaring visitors brought many invasives, mostly animals, such as the smooth-billed ani, a black bird that was meant to remove ticks from cattle but ended up preying on baby lizards, nearly pushing them to extinction. Cats and rats also jumped off early cargo ships leading to the extinction of bird species.

Exotic species invasions do seem to affect islands more. Hawaii is well known for high numbers of invasive species. It is difficult to know if it is an issue of a small ecosystem or the result of a high number of exotics simply being accidentally introduced. If either scenario is true, then perhaps islands are more vulnerable. One thing is clear, however—no easy equation exists to determine an ecosystem's vulnerability to exotics.

*Alan Burdick. "The Truth About Invasive Species." *Discover* 26, no. 5 (May 2005): pp. 34–41.

Giant salvinia has horizontal rhizomes and a third leaf that dangles below the water's surface. Although floating-leaved plants generally use water for support, this third leaf helps to stabilize the plant because it tends to grow to great lengths. Another feature that enables giant salvinia to thrive in its aquatic environment is the rows of white bristly hairs that help to repel water.

## Giant Salvinia Management

On August 4, 1999, some staff members of the U. S. Fish and Wildlife Service watched the disheartening sight of giant salvinia floating down the Colorado River in the Cibola National Wildlife Refuge in Pretty Water and Three Finger Lake. With the reputation of giant salvinia being the world's worst aquatic weed, the Lower Colorado Task Force formed with the ambitious goal of eradication. The source of the infestation was determined, and a barrier was placed to prevent further spread. Intensive herbicide applications began, and progress is being monitored. This innovative task force has transcended national borders and focuses on boundaries that weeds are familiar with—waterways.

Biological control provides a long-term control option versus a short-term fix. Much success has been shown with an imported weevil, *Crytobagous salviniae*, originally from South America (Figure 5.2). The salvinia weevil causes immense damage to plants by tunneling through rhizomes and feeding on the latent buds that would otherwise become new plants. This type of injury helps to keep giant salvinia from growing vastly out of control.

This weevil has been released in Texas and Louisiana in just the last few years. Scientists are studying the release sites and recording on both the insect and plant. The insects will be evaluated for survival and reproduction rates. These weevils usually produce one generation per year. Plant damage will also be assessed. Generally in a successful biological control release, the insects are not only found to survive and reproduce but spread beyond the release site. A growing weevil population should lead to a decrease in invasive plant biomass. (**Biomass** is the total amount of living plant material.)

## AN ESCAPED ORNAMENTAL: WATER HYACINTH

Water hyacinth (*Eichhornia crassipes*) rivals giant salvinia as one of the worst weeds. Until fairly recently, this invasive aquatic plant covered as much as 125,000 acres of water in Florida. Many lakes and ponds were covered from shore to shore with this South American native. Hyacinth, similar to giant salvinia, has a frightening growth rate; it can double its population in as little as 12 days.

**Figure 5.3**  The beauty of the water hyacinth's flower is one of the reasons for its continued spread. It still is sold as an ornamental in some states.

## Water Hyacinth Cleans Up

One of the qualities that makes the water hyacinth such a nuisance plant is now being harnessed to clean wastewater or sewage. Hyacinth is a rapid grower. Rapid growers have high nutrient needs and floating-leaved plants get their nutrients from the water. Oddly enough, sewage is a source of nutrients. The hyacinth is able to absorb and digest these repulsive compounds and make the water cleaner. As a result, these waters do encourage the growth of hyacinth. Luckily the hyacinth can be harvested for use as fertilizer since it is so nutrient rich after sucking up all that sewage. Another long-range possibility is using the heat-treated form of hyacinth to produce methane for energy.

In Rio Hondo, Texas, water hyacinth has been successfully used to treat sewage. The town decided to dig a lagoon and import hyacinths instead of building a sewage treatment plant that would have cost 20 times more than the hyacinth-filled lagoon.

Water hyacinth was likely introduced intentionally during the 1884 Cotton States Exposition in New Orleans. Because of its beautiful flowers, water hyacinth is still sold as an ornamental for small fish ponds where it often escapes from cultivation (Figure 5.3).

Hyacinth leaves are connected by modified stems referred to as **stolons**. Stolons are stems that grow horizontally along the ground surface. Stolons that are broken and contain a node or joint can produce a new plant. Producing a new plant from a piece of root is known as vegetative reproduction, and water hyacinth is able to quickly colonize large areas. The free-floating nature of this weed also enables it to relocate based on wind and water currents. Water hyacinth also reproduces sexually with the production of seeds that are able to withstand long periods of drought, remaining dormant until there is another period of flooding.

## Water Hyacinth Management

Once established, eradication of water hyacinth is too lofty of a goal; reducing the weed to levels that will allow humans, fish, and animals to use the pond or lake is realistic. In Florida, water hyacinth has been reduced to reasonable levels by combining herbicides and mechanical methods on an annual basis. Skipping even just one year of control can undo all previous efforts and can result in millions of dollars in additional costs to return to maintenance levels.

# 6

# Invasive Submersed Plants

• • • • • • • • • • • • • • • • • • • • • • • • •

Invasive submersed plants interfere with human activity. They clog irrigation waterways, block the flow of shallow streams, and inhibit recreational water activities.

## A BOAT CASTAWAY: HYDRILLA

In Washington State, a canoe ventures to the middle of a lake. With the weather cooperating for many of the summer weekends, canoeists have the opportunity to visit many lakes during the season. Once out in the middle of this pristine lake, Mary notices a dark green, shiny piece of vegetation not even a half inch (1.25 centimeters) long in the bottom of the canoe, probably previously stuck on the paddle from last weekend's trip. A slightly withered and innocent-looking piece of a plant, Mary decides to throw it into the water. This small fragment of hydrilla will be the source of ecological devastation for this aquatic community.

This piece of plant material was actually a **turion**, which is a compact bud produced along the leafy hydrilla stems. Turions as small as one-quarter inch (.6 cm) can produce a new plant and can withstand ice cover, drying, herbicides, and ingestion and regurgitation by waterfowl (Figure 6.1). **Tubers** are another clever way that hydrilla reigns in the aquatic world. Tubers are underground and form at the end of roots. A tuber is a modified root; a potato is an example of a tuber. The tubers from hydrilla resemble tiny potatoes, usually white or yellowish. One square meter of hydrilla can produce 5,000 tubers. In addition to its strength as a prolific vegetative propagator, hydrilla can also grow

**Figure 6.1** Hydrilla is easily spread from one water body to another by boat propellers. Hydrilla plant parts called turions that are as small as one-quarter inch can become a new plant.

in lower light conditions and is generally more efficient in taking up nutrients than other plants.

Hydrilla was brought to Florida in the 1960s from Africa or Asia through the aquarium trade. Hydrilla forms dense mats that limit recreational use of bodies of water as well as destroy fish and wildlife habitats. Water delivery systems are affected as well. This plant has become such a nuisance in southern states that in Florida an estimated $56 million has been spent on hydrilla control during a ten-year period. Hydrilla has also made its way to California where an aggressive eradication program is underway.

## Hydrilla Management

In places where hydrilla has not yet become widespread, eradication is still a realistic goal. In Washington, hydrilla was discovered in two interconnected privately owned lakes near Seattle. Divers surveyed nearby lakes to see if the hydrilla had spread. It appeared that they had not, and by using the appropriate management techniques, hydrilla has not spread beyond the original infestation area.

Hydrilla can be controlled with aquatic herbicides. Grass carp can also be used to consume hydrilla. Control efforts must be repeated and sites must be continually monitored since hydrilla tubers are long-lived and will not all sprout at once.

Luckily, hydrilla is not being sold today so the deliberate influx of this aquatic weed is not as great as other invasive aquatics. Managing aquatic invasive plants consists of not only struggling to control what is already here but prevention of new infestations.

## FROM AQUARIUMS TO THE GREAT LAKES: EURASIAN WATERMILFOIL

Eurasian watermilfoil (*Myriophyllum spicatum*) is a submersed rooted perennial aquatic weed with stems that extend as much as 33 feet (10 meters) in length and form dense mats (Figure 6.2). The flower-bearing portion of the plant is actually above water but produces little seed. Similar to other aquatic weeds that form dense mats, Eurasian watermilfoil destroys fish and wildlife habitats as well as native aquatic plant life. The stems of this weed are slender and branching, and contain leaflets that give milfoil a signature feathery appearance. This plant grows so

**Figure 6.2** Eurasian watermilfoil is a rooted perennial with a feathery appearance. This submersed invasive provides little food to wildlife and yet crowds out valuable native plants with its dense mats.

rapidly that lakes, rivers, and other water bodies become thick with dense milfoil mats where light is not able to penetrate the surface. Milfoil is rarely used for food by wildlife and generally slows water to the point of increasing the breeding of mosquitoes. Dense milfoil mats prevent proper spawning of fish. While dense cover is adequate for young fish, larger predatory fish lose foraging space and have a difficult time finding their prey.

Eurasian watermilfoil thrives in areas of natural and man-made disturbance. It is also tolerant of pollutants. Nearly all states have been invaded by this native of Eurasia and Africa. It is abundant in the Chesapeake Bay, the tidal Potomac River, and several Tennessee Valley reservoirs.

No one really knows how Eurasian watermilfoil got here in the 1940s but one theory is that it escaped from an aquarium. Another possibility is that it was inadvertently introduced by attachment to a commercial or private boat.

Eurasian watermilfoil is able to colonize a variety of habitats, including fresh and brackish water. It can also tolerate low water temperatures that allow earlier spring growth than other aquatic plants. Milfoil dominates by dispersal of plant fragments into lakes, streams, and water currents into drainage areas. Pieces of milfoil stuck on motorboats are a troublesome source of spread because new infestations can easily occur. Road checks in Minnesota have found aquatic vegetation on 23% of all trailered watercraft inspected.

## Eurasian Watermilfoil Management

Prevention is always the best method of control for such a devastating invasive aquatic plant. Because of the difficulty in properly identifying aquatic plants, the transport of any aquatic vegetation is now illegal in Minnesota and Washington. Other prevention measures include citizen lake-watcher programs, boat cleaning programs, professional survey programs, boat launch surveillance, educational approaches such as workshops and lectures, and Web sites. Measures such as these are inexpensive and can go far in preventing costly weed control or entirely losing a lake to milfoil.

Herbicides and mechanical removal provide adequate, immediate control but must be followed up every one to three years. Handcutting tools are effective on submersed milfoil. The main problem is that cutting, if not done properly, could increase the amount of milfoil because it increases the number of plant fragments. Removed milfoil will need to be disposed of in a place where there is no chance that pieces could be washed back into a water body; a dry, upland site is preferable. Rotovation is another mechanical control technique where the root crown that lies in the sediment is targeted for removal. Rotovation is similar to tillage where both the crown and associated plant tissue are removed. The problem is that rotovation may damage the sediment and some states have prohibited it.

Biological control by introducing insects or pathogens installs a more sustained control method but currently there are no approved biological control agents for water milfoil. *Mycoleptodiscus terrestris*, a fungal pathogen, is under research for use as a contact bioherbicide. Interestingly, this pathogen is native, not from the same location as the milfoil. When in contact with this pathogen, plants rapidly fall apart but can regrow from the roots. The advantages are that many other weeds are affected, which also presents the disadvantage of injuring native vegetation. Another disadvantage is inconsistent effectiveness.

A few insects are being investigated as biological control agents: a moth (*Acentria ephemerella*), a tiny fly called a midge

## Making Polluters Pay:
## Resource-to-Resource Compensation

Most states fine polluters to compensate for natural resources that have been damaged. Another approach developed in the state of New Jersey is referred to as resource-to-resource compensation where polluters voluntarily choose to purchase an equivalent amount of land for preservation and recreation as was damaged to compensate residents for prior damage to the environment. Resource-to-resource compensation avoids costly litigation and complex, time-consuming monetary evaluations of natural resource injuries focusing on restoration and land preservation projects.

One of the largest natural resource damage settlements in New Jersey's history was settled in this fashion. In 2005, New Jersey's Department of Environmental Protection (DEP) reached an agreement with E. I. DuPont de Nemours and Company ("DuPont") to compensate the public for injuries to groundwater at eight hazardous sites in New Jersey. DuPont manufactures chemicals, energy, and

(*Cricotopus myriophyll*), and a weevil (*Euhrychiopsis lecontei*). The caterpillar of *Acentria ephemerella* has been in North America since the 1920s and is a consumer of aquatic macrophytes. Results have been mixed with the best declines of milfoil from this insect in New York. In the Midwest, the caterpillar has not attained high enough densities to have an impact on the milfoil. The midge has been successful in the Pacific Northwest in reducing milfoil densities but mass rearing of the tiny insect is difficult.

The most promising option is the weevil, which is native to North America and a specialist herbivore of watermilfoils, meaning that it prefers milfoil to other aquatic vegetation. When materials including plastics and pesticides. The settlement includes preservation of 1,875 acres of land, planting of 3,000 trees in urban areas, payment of $500,000 to the state for water restoration projects, and construction of a boat ramp along a recreational river.

DuPont approached the state willing to settle its natural resource damage claim for contaminating 2,400 acres of groundwater. In the resource-to-resource compensation model, DuPont had to protect an equivalent area of land with a high aquifer recharge rate (the rate at which water percolates in to replace groundwater). Since DuPont only offered 1,875 acres as compensation, DEP required additional environmental projects to make up for the acreage difference. DuPont will provide $1.8 million for urban shade tree plantings. DuPont will also provide $500,000 to restore wetland habitat or purchase aquifer recharge areas in addition to the lands that DuPont itself is purchasing.

choosing a biological control agent, food preference is critical. For one, there is a danger that desirable vegetation could be injured if the insect doesn't have a strong preference for the invasive plant. Adult weevils live underwater and lay eggs that eventually hatch; the larvae then eat the milfoil. This injury results in suppressed milfoil plant growth and reduced root growth and carbohydrate stores, and often causes the plant to sink from the top of the water surface to the bottom. Predation by sunfish is one known factor that inhibits the success of the weevil. Although the weevil is the most promising of all the potential biological control agents, results are still mixed and therefore research is ongoing.

# 7 Invasive Aquatic and Wetland Plant Management

W eed management plans are created on both large and small scales. A small-scale management plan would be the decision to use fire and herbicides to control weeds in a 10-acre preserve. Weed management plans for thousand-acre national forests or statewide plans are also crucial yet serve a different function. Large-scale weed management plans have the additional challenge of discovering all of the weeds that may need control. The initial focus in large-scale plans is identification and proper mapping.

Natural resource managers must evaluate many criteria when they decide what method to use. The intended use of the water should be considered. In many cases, it may not be necessary to completely eradicate all unwanted vegetation. If enough of the vegetation is removed to enable the wetland or aquatic area to be restored for its former use, this is likely to suffice. If a highly invasive aquatic plant has newly invaded a pond, a policy of complete eradication is typical.

The method for use should be evaluated for its potential hazards to the ecosystem and people. An alteration in the aquatic environment could result in severe damage to fish and desirable plants. Cost and effectiveness should also be evaluated.

## BURNING

In the semiarid environment of Larimer County, Colorado, hay farmers rely on irrigation to grow their crops. With irrigation, they can have three cuttings of hay per season; without it, only one. The precious water for irrigation is brought to a farmer named Ken's land through irrigation ditches. During summer the irrigation ditches flow with water, and as the fall approaches, the ditches are again empty—almost. The abundance of water has attracted leafy spurge (*Euphorbia esula*).

Leafy spurge grows in rangelands, wetlands, and roadsides, and spreads primarily by waterways because the seeds float. A toxic perennial, it has the ability to displace native vegetation, devastate wildlife habitat, and cause economic loss to rangeland.

Leafy spurge is one of the biggest threats to the Poudre River ecosystem, which is the source of irrigation for Ken's farm. According to natural resource professionals, approximately 50,000 acres of spurge occupies Larimer County.

This plant is native to Russia and is believed to have been accidentally introduced into the United States as a contaminant in hay in the 1800s. In the process of this introduction, the natural predator that keeps the plant in control was left behind.

Even though it is fall and the growing season is winding down, Ken knows how important it is that he remove the leafy spurge from the ditches. As a perennial, the plant will grow dormant and a healthy crop will resprout in the early spring. Burning will help stress the plant and remove it from the ditches.

Ken gathers help to do his annual burn. He uses a drip-torch to ignite the strip of weeds and a water tank with a spray gun to extinguish it. The aboveground growth of leafy spurge is gone as the final flames are drenched with water. The roots underground remain healthy and are able to resprout. Ken knows this but his goal of clearing his ditches until next season has been accomplished.

Burning is a tool in weed management, even in aquatic areas, if there are dry periods. Burning is often used to remove weeds when no desirable species are present and where the weedy vegetation has grown so thick that access is difficult, particularly along waterways. Burning also works well in combination with herbicides. Resprouting will occur with biennials or perennials but the new growth will be more susceptible to herbicides.

## HAND-HARVESTING

In 1996, Eurasian watermilfoil was discovered in the 5,200-acre Upper Saranac Lake near Adirondack Park, New York. Local residents become concerned and rallied to use benthic barriers and hand-harvesting by four divers. Aquatic herbicides were not used due to political pressures. The three-year effort yielded 50 acres of extracted milfoil at a cost of approximately $60,000

### Insect Releases: Deciding How Many

In Arapahoe County, Colorado, an estimated 5,000 acres of leafy spurge continue to spread. Arapahoe County wanted a long-term solution to the leafy spurge problem and released leafy spurge flea beetles. They did not want to wait the traditional three to eight years to see significant results so they released much larger numbers of the insects instead of the typical 500 to 1,000 insects per site.

In 1999, 55,000 insects were released in Cherry Creek State Park. In 2000, an additional 45,000 insects were released at a different site. Insects are quite expensive if purchased privately, usually $1 per insect. Arapahoe County staff members were able to collect insects for free by going to the Leafy Spurge Festival in North Dakota.

With initial releases this high, significant reductions in leafy spurge were visible by the next season. In addition, many of the annually. Although impressive, these efforts were not enough to prevent spread or reestablishment of the weed. A more aggressive hand-harvesting program was implemented in 2004.

Twenty divers were trained in watermilfoil identification, removal, and underwater safety. Divers hand-pulled Eurasian watermilfoil systematically around the lake and tracked the weed infestations using global positioning system (GPS) units, recorded detailed information about native plants present, and bagged and then transported the milfoil. Other resources used were 10 "top-water" team members, four dive platform boats, two tank dive boats, dinghies, kayaks, and a patrol boat. Divers worked five days a week for nearly two months.

native plants had come back once released from competition with the leafy spurge.

The best places to use the insects are in areas with good drainage, low traffic, moderate density of spurge, and south-facing slopes. The best soil type is a silt clay loam with some organic matter because it generally promotes shallow lateral root systems.

Cherry Creek State Park will be used to collect and redistribute the insects to other leafy spurge sites throughout Arapahoe County. Collection and sorting of insects is done by sweeping the release areas once insects have had a chance to establish. In the process of sweeping, generally 95 percent of insects fall back to the group so over-collecting is not a problem. The best time to sweep is 10 A.M. to 4 P.M. on sunny days. Insects are placed in a sorter and then put in a breathable but sealed container and placed in a refrigerator.

Benthic barriers were also placed on the lake bottom. Benthic barriers are natural or synthetic materials used to cover plants on the bottom of the lake, pond, or reservoir; plants usually die within one month underneath the barrier. The project cost approximately $535,000 in 2004 at a cost of about $200 per acre of infestation.

Since this is a three-year project, results are not yet available. Project leaders believe this program will show that hand-harvesting can be effective at controlling even large-scale milfoil infestations, but control in large or heavily infested lakes requires significant resources and a well-devised plan of attack.[16]

The project at Upper Saranac Lake is an example of a mechanical approach where there is removal of all or part of the plant, varying from hand-pulling to the use of specialized rakes and cutters. Community cleanup days or weed-pulling events are popular in recreational areas. Hand-pulling is most effective on annuals but can also be used for perennials if follow-up monitoring and subsequent removal is planned. Biennials and perennials will resprout, however, and all plants have viable seeds that can germinate at a later time. The advantage of hand-pulling is that desirable plants do not get accidentally injured unless someone misidentifies a desirable plant as an invasive plant. Hand-pulling is advantageous when perhaps only one or two invasive plants need to be removed, as opposed to acres of weeds.

More sophisticated equipment can be used to remove aquatic vegetation. Units range from toothed blades that attach to a rowboat to large harvesters equipped with retrieval and uploading conveyors.[17] Equipment such as this can remove large quantities of aquatic vegetation and is quite beneficial where overgrowth has reduced available oxygen levels. Grinders or juicers are also used to cut and grind weeds in the lake. Unfortunately the plant parts can again become suspended and decaying plant material in the lake can reduce available oxygen and become a nuisance.

Harvesters can also be used to increase the effectiveness of a herbicide application. If unwanted aquatic vegetation is cut and then allowed to grow for another week or so, the weeds will be much more sensitive to the herbicide in their regrowth stage. Often, natural resource managers prefer to use more than one management strategy to improve results.

Harvesting is futile unless all plant parts are bagged and removed from the body of water; otherwise they will reestablish. Also, mobility is restricted around shorelines and some areas may not be easily accessed. Weeds that are dredged have to be hauled away for disposal, and this can be costly since fresh, wet weeds can be quite heavy.

## BIOLOGICAL CONTROL
To battle leafy spurge, the Larimer County Parks and Open Lands Department offers insects for free to landowners that have leafy spurge. Flea beetles control leafy spurge by feeding on the foliage during their adult stage and feeding on the roots during the larval stage. Significant changes in vegetation may take three to eight years, assuming that the initial insect population survives and continues to reproduce. Flea beetles will migrate up to one mile to other leafy spurge populations, but human intervention can speed up the process.

These insects have undergone extensive research by the U.S. Department of Agriculture-Animal and Plant Health Inspection Service (USDA-APHIS) to ensure that desirable plant species will not be affected. Leafy spurge flea beetles are host-specific, meaning that they will eat only leafy spurge. These beetles will not eat garden flowers or other desirable plants. They also will not bite people, pets, or livestock.

**Figure 7.1** Carp are stocked in a lake to control unwanted vegetation. Fish screens allow the passage of desirable fish such as trout, but contain the carp so that they will eat the undesirable plants.

Biological control is generally more popular with the public since it does not use chemicals. Risks to the environment still exist for this control strategy. Even so, herbivores (plant eaters), microbial bioaugmentation, plant pathogens (diseases), and competitive species are all continually being evaluated to control unwanted aquatic and wetland vegetation. Natural insect predators, specifically moths and weevils, in both the adult and larval stage do selectively feed on invasive aquatic plants. Success has been shown in controlling water hyacinth and Eurasian watermilfoil. Plant diseases or pathogens can be used to control vegetation and include bacteria, viruses, fungi, and other microorganisms that infect aquatic plants. Again, there is always the concern of affecting native vegetation.

Plant-eating fish such as a sterile form of white amur grass carp (*Ctenopharyngodon idella*) have been used in lakes, ponds, and canals with some controversy (Figure 7.1). Some states have banned their introduction because the effects on native fish are unknown. These fish do well at consuming vegetation and there is some evidence that they have a preference for hydrilla, but they will eventually consume other types of growth when the unwanted vegetation becomes scarce. Another concern is that the short intestine of the fish does not fully digest the plant matter and causes a rapid return of nutrients to the water and a subsequent algal bloom.

Microbial bioaugmentation adds naturally occurring micro-organisms and enzymes to accelerate organic decomposition and to create or augment an essential component of an ecosystem's food web.[18] Essentially, complex organic matter is broken down by these organisms and is then available as food for other aquatic life. Gases are produced as by-products of the decomposition and are either released into the air or are assimilated into the microorganism itself. With all of these control measures however, it is important to look at the source of unwanted growth.

Evaluating watershed management practices that contribute to eutrophication of a water body is a more effective way to deal with the problem. Eutrophication is the enrichment of a lake or pond by nutrients that increase photosynthetic productivity. Adding microorganisms will not have much of an impact unless the source of nutrients is reduced.

## DRAWDOWN

Drawdown is when water levels are lowered to expose sediments and subsequently dry out vegetation. This method can only be used for man-made lakes or regulated rivers with a dam or water control structure. Burning can then be used as well. In the winter, the ground will freeze and kill roots and underground

### Can This Wetland Be Saved?

Before the reign of Saddam Hussein, the wetlands in the middle and lower basin of the Tigris and Euphrates rivers in Iraq were the most extensive wetlands in the Middle East. These Mesopotamian wetlands consisted of shallow marshes covered in reeds where the groundwater was at or above the ground surface. They were a crucial winter stop for migratory birds and waterfowl and a nursery for shrimp; the wetlands also purified agricultural pollutants before they flowed into the Persian Gulf. And then came war.

The Iran-Iraq War (1980–1988) took place in much of the wetlands and involved extensive burning, bombing and shelling, and the use of chemical weapons. The fires burned so hot that the mineralogy of the soil was changed. Then, in the 1990s, the Iraqi government drained the wetlands because the region was believed to be a hiding place for deserters and dissidents. Whether these wetlands can be restored is the question for ecologists and development aid agencies.

stems. If fish are present, drawdown is obviously not desirable. As with most management strategies, the problem of viable seeds still exists.

## REVEGETATION

Damage to a wetland is difficult to undo. Ecosystems are resilient and can tolerate a certain amount of disturbance without turning into a wasteland. Once a wetland has stopped functioning, meaning that it no longer does the things a wetland does—purify water and provide habitat and food for animals— restoration is much more difficult.

Take for example the difference between these two forms of disturbance: damming of a water source that feeds a wetland

The first step was restoring the source of water to the wetlands by blowing up dikes. Revegetation and monitoring of pollutants is the next. After the reflooding, black ooze floated on top of the water; other areas have high levels of sulfur, chlorides, and sodium.

Some of the marshes have done remarkably well and have been restored to their former functions. One of the marshes 30 miles (48 kilometers) north of Nasiriyah is now replete with phytoplankton, aquatic plants, mollusks, freshwater fish, and 31 species of birds, 3 of which are endangered. Marshes that received heavy doses of pollutants are coming back more slowly. Species of fish that once thrived in these marshes are present in low numbers, making the lives of Iraqis in this area very difficult. Many have not yet been able to return to the land. Whether this region can return to its full former capacity remains to be seen, but the wetlands' resilience has already been remarkable.

and intense grazing by cows along a wetland. The first form of disturbance will likely alter wetland functions. Restoration would require not only an alternative source of water (if even possible) but likely the revegetation of wetland plants that have probably died. Intense grazing, assuming that the land has not been completely denuded, is a less destructive form of disturbance, and all that may be needed is the removal of some of the grazing animals. The difference between the two has far-reaching implications as to the restoration steps involved or if restoration is even possible.

Both types of disturbance described above leave the ecosystem vulnerable to invasive aquatic and wetland plant species. Any restoration project requires an immediate assessment of invasive plants. Once the weeds are controlled, it is important to fill the previously weedy spots with desirable vegetation. If left bare, invasive species will return to the aquatic region. **Revegetation** is the process of putting back desirable plants with seeds, seedlings, or mature plants. Species chosen should be desirable (primarily native) plants and species that are known to be competitive to the weed.

Even with the best efforts to control invasive plant species from the area, viable seeds will be left that can germinate and become new invasive plants. Revegetation aims to seed with enough desirable plants that the weed seeds that germinate will not dominate again. Unfortunately there is no way to kill ungerminated weed seeds, with the exception of an extremely high-temperature fire; however, the temperature required would also result in damage to the sediment.

## AQUATIC HERBICIDES

Although often publicly unfavorable, aquatic herbicides are often the cheapest and most effective way to control invasive aquatic and wetland plants. For nearly two decades, the EPA, which is responsible for approving pesticides, has required that all aquatic herbicides must have less than a one in a million chance of causing significant harmful effects to human health, wildlife, or the environment. Therefore, herbicides labeled for aquatic use are limited in number, but applicators can feel confident in using them safely.

In treating submersed species, application is made directly to the water and the plants take up the herbicide from the water. Floating and emergent species would be sprayed directly with a herbicide to the vegetative surface.

Herbicides are generally categorized as systemic or contact. Systemic herbicides are applied to the foliage or roots, and the plant-killing chemical is translocated or moved throughout the weed. Systemic herbicides are preferred for perennials because the chemical will move through the roots, which are the most tenacious parts of a weed. Contact herbicides cause injury to the weed exactly where they touch the plant. Contact herbicides do not move throughout the plant.

## THE ECOSYSTEM OF THE FUTURE

The issue of invasive species is garnering more and more recognition and will be just as well known an environmental topic as the hole in the ozone layer or global warming. As with any environmental crisis, there are naysayers. Some argue that invasive species are an example of ecology simply becoming more globalized, just like society. People are not inhibited by geographic boundaries so it only makes sense that plants would follow suit.

Others even argue whether invasive species truly damage the ecosystem or merely cause a species shift. It has been argued that ecosystems can merely take on these additional exotic species;

ecosystems are not filled with a finite number of jobs or niches as previously thought but rather native species could move aside and simply make room for the exotics. This book has aimed to demonstrate the shortcomings of these thoughts.

## Do-It-Yourself Land Management

It's relatively easy to control weeds in a moderately sized backyard. Maintaining property that is communally owned gets a little more tricky. A park or creek can easily get neglected by a municipality. The individuals responsible for maintaining the property may have dozens more that are in need of critical attention—new restrooms or a busted fence and that new crop of purple loosestrife may go unnoticed. The naturalist who takes his morning walk along the creek may notice a new invasive plant or eroded riverbank. What should a concerned individual do?

Resources are available for individuals who care for lands that they do not directly own. The Center for Invasive Plant Management (http://www.weedcenter.org) offers grants typically in the amount of $5,000 for weed control projects. In Dubois, Idaho, private citizens and public land permittees partnered in a project referred to as the Continental Divide Weed Management Area. The project aimed to protect their watershed from leafy spurge.

Idaho's Camas Creek watershed includes high mountains, high mountain meadows, forests, high desert, and valley meadow land used for native and alfalfa hay production. Nearly all of it is above 6,000 feet (1,800 meters) in elevation. The primary weeds of concern are leafy spurge and spotted knapweed *(Centaurea maculosa)*, which are found in abundance in nearby drainages. The Camas area is still relatively free of these weeds, although several isolated infestations have been found. The primary purpose of this project is to find pre-

It is not enough to say that these exotic species just don't belong. And yet it is difficult to quantify the losses in an ecosystem from invasive species. It is much easier to point to wetlands filled with gravel and sand in preparation for

viously undiscovered infestations and eradicate them before they become too large to eradicate.

Participants described their project accordingly: When the leafy spurge was in bloom, the Eagle Rock Backcountry Horsemen, equipped with global positioning system (GPS) units, rode the area searching for infestations. They recorded the coordinates for the infestations they found. Two herbicide spray units on pack animals were taken into the areas where infestations were previously found. ATV (all-terrain vehicle) units were used in accessible areas. The infestations were mapped using GPS units and treated with an appropriate herbicide. The sites will be revisited in the fall to determine whether a complete kill was achieved, and follow-up treatment will be made if necessary. The sites will be monitored in the summer of the next year and again treated if necessary. Participants in the Continental Divide Weed Management Area project were given $5,000 to carry out this project.

Local agencies such as county weed districts generally offer information on identification and management of weeds. In some cases, financial assistance is also available through a cost-share program for insects, herbicides, cultural control, and mowing used to control noxious weeds. Landowners can borrow GPS equipment to map their weeds. Backpack sprayers and 25-gallon sprayers are also available for loan. Landowners with a considerable leafy spurge infestation can receive free biological control agents.

a condo complex, shake one's head sadly, and say "What a tragedy" than to comprehend the force of change from an invasive species explosion. When the last lavender-flowered columbine (*Aquilegra ssp.*) dies from lack of water, defeated by a monoculture of deep-rooted Russian knapweed in a quiet Rocky Mountain foothill, there is no visible destruction of fallen trees from deforestation or exhaust of smelly fumes from diesel-powered bulldozers to offend the senses. There isn't the same sense of fallen grandeur as a heap of giant sequoias. Death is silent, but the loss is just as significant. Not only do we lose species from the invasion of exotics but we also lose the use of our beloved wetlands, lakes, and ponds. The loss is palpable for those residents whose local lake has been invaded by Eurasian watermilfoil: no more canoeing, no more swimming, no more fishing. Invasive species can dramatically change the quality of our lives, and that's why it is important for individuals and communities to work together to control their spread.

# NOTES

1. Osha Gray Davidson, *The Enchanted Braid: Coming to Terms With Nature on the Coral Reef.* New York: John Wiley and Sons, 1998, p. 3.

2. Lynn Margulis, *Symbiotic Planet.* Amherst, MA: Basic Books, 1998, p. 110.

3. E. O. Wilson, *The Diversity of Life.* Cambridge, MA: Harvard University Press, 1992, p. 141.

4. Kenneth L. Gosner, *Atlantic Seashore: A field guide to sponges, jellyfish, sea urchins, and more.* New York: Houghton Mifflin Company, 1978, p. 17.

5. Ibid., p. 19.

6. J. R. Singleton, "Production and utilization of waterfowl food plants on the east Texas gulf coast," *Journal of Wildlife Management* 15, no. 1 (1951): 46–56.

7. Wilson, *The Diversity of Life*, p. 94.

8. Jonathan Silvertown, "Plant phenotypic plasticity and non-cognitive behavior," *Trends in Ecology and Evolution* 13, (1998): 255–256.Available on line at: http://cas.bellarmine.edu/tietjen/Ecology/plant_phenotypic_plasticity_and_.htm.

9. Ibid.

10. Ibid.

11. D. Q. Thompson and R. L. Stuckey. "Spread, Impact, and Control of Purple Loosestrife (*Lythrum Salicaria*) in North American Wetlands. The Case for Biological Control," Available online at: http://www.npwrc.usgs.gov/resource/1999/loosstrf.

12. Ibid.

13. Ibid.

14. C. C. Jacono, *"Giant Salvinia."* USGS, 2003. Available online at: http://salvinia.er.usgs.gov/html/identification.html.

15. Ibid.

16. M.R. Martin and C. Stiles, "The Use of Hand-harvesting to Control Eurasian Milfoil in Upper Saranac Lake, Franklin County, NY," Presentation at the NEAPMS annual conference, Saratoga Springs, NY, 2005. Available online at: http://www.cayugalake.org/DSL/Chapt6aAq_Plt_Mngmnt_Case_Studies050412.doc.

17. Applied Biochemists. "Aquatic Plant Problems," *Land and Water Magazine* 46, no. 1 (2000). Available online at: http://www.landandwater.com/features/vol46no1_1.html.

18. Ibid.

# GLOSSARY

**Adaptation**   Small change in a species that causes a genetic variation and increases an organism's ability to survive.

**Aerenchyma**   Intracellular spaces that aquatic plants rely on to supply oxygen.

**Angiosperm**   Flowering plant that produces seeds.

**Annelid**   Animal, such as a leech, that has a segmented body.

**Balanoid**   Refers to barnacles.

**Balanoid-thallophyte**   A habitat where organisms need to have something to attach to, such as a rocky shore. Such organisms include barnacles and seaweeds, as well as brightly colored lichen that appear above the water zone and are tolerant of occasional mists of salt water.

**Ballast water**   Water that ships take up to maintain stability during transport; this water usually contains stow-away organisms.

**Biomass**   The total amount of living plant material.

**Bog**   Freshwater wetland, often formed in old glacial lakes, characterized by spongy peat deposits, evergreen trees and shrubs, and a floor covered by a thick carpet of sphagnum moss.

**Brackish**   Describes an area where freshwater and salt water mix.

**Climax community**   A mature ecosystem where all interacting organisms are stable and in balance with one another.

**Ecosystem**   The interdependence of living organisms and their environment.

**Emergent plant**   Plant that is rooted in the sediment, but the top of the plant extends into the air.

**Emersed plant**   Plant that rises above the surface of the water.

**Fen**   Freshwater peat-forming wetland covered mostly by grasses, sedges, reeds, and wildflowers.

**Free-floating plant**   Plant that floats at or just below the water's surface with roots that do not extend into the sediment below.

**Generalist species**   Plants that can live in a wide variety of environments. Most nonnative plants that are invasive are generalists.

**Gymnosperm**   Plant that produces spores for reproduction.

**High tide zone**   The part of the littoral zone that is flooded during high tide.

**Host-specific**   Refers to biological control insects that will only attack one plant or host.

**Intertidal**   The area between the highest and lowest tides.

**Invasive species**   Animals, plants, and microbes that infiltrate and invade ecosystems beyond their historic range.

**Littoral zone**   The area where aquatic, rooted plants will grow along a shore or lake between the highest and lowest tides.

**Lower littoral zone** or **low tide zone**   The deepest part of the water where submersed plants can still grow.

**Macronutrient**   Nutrient that plants need in large quantities.

**Marsh**   Wetland dominated by soft-stemmed vegetation.

**Micronutrient**   Nutrient that plants need in smaller amounts.

**Middle tide zone**   That part of the littoral zone where plants are covered and uncovered with water daily.

**Monoculture**   A plant community made up of a single species.

**Pelagic**   Habitat within the ocean biome that consists of plants and animals that float or drift free with the plankton.

**Pelecypod**   Refers to animals that have a shell, such as a clam.

**Pelecypod-annelid**   A biome that consists of unconsolidated sediments. These soft grounds have varying textures depending on particle size and then classified as sand, silt, or clay. Many of the organisms that live here are burrowers.

**Phenotypic plasticity**   The variation between individual plants of the same species growing in different environments.

**Phytoplankton**   Minute plantlike organisms that are the energy-producing tenants in a lake or pond.

**Pioneer species**   Plants that are first to arrive, usually after a disturbance such as fire, flood, or volcanic eruption.

**Revegetation**   The process of putting back desirable plants with seeds, seedlings, or mature plants.

**Rhizome**   Modified stem that spreads horizontally underground; often informally referred to as creeping roots.

**Siltation**   The process where a waterway accumulates greater amounts of silt.

**Specialist species**   Plants with very specific roles in an ecosystem.

**Sporocarp**   Outer sac on a fern that contains numerous sporangia. Sporangia are the equivalent of seeds in flowering plants.

**Spray zone**   Also called the upper littoral zone; the part of the littoral zone that is dry most of the time.

**Stolon**   Stem that grows horizontally along the ground surface.

**Stomate**   Opening on leaves through which terrestrial plants exchange gases that they need, such as carbon dioxide and oxygen.

**Submersed plant**   Plant that is completely underwater.

**Succession**   The gradual replacement of one set of plant species for another.

**Thallophyte**   Describes plants that absorb their food over a growing surface, such as a rocky shore.

**Tuber**   A modified root that is underground; a potato is a tuber.

**Turion**   A compact bud produced along leafy stems. Turions as small as one-quarter inch can produce a new plant. They can withstand ice cover, drying, herbicides, and ingestion and regurgitation by waterfowl.

**Water column**   The "cylinder" of water from the surface of the water body to the bottom.

# BIBLIOGRAPHY

Applied Biochemists. "Aquatic Plant Problems." *Land and Water Magazine* 146, no. 6 (2000).

Attenborough, David. *The Private Life of Plants*. Princeton, N.J.: Princeton University Press, 1995.

Burdick, Alan. "The Truth About Invasive Species." *Discover* 26, no. 5 (May 2005): pp. 34–41.

Davidson, Osha Gray. *The Enchanted Braid: Coming to Terms with Nature on the Coral Reef*. New York: John Wiley and Sons, 1998.

Filson, R. P. "Island Biogeography and Evolution: Solving a Phylogenetic Puzzle Using Molecular Genetics." University of California, Berkeley—Museum of Paleontology. Available online at: http://www.ucmp.berk eey.edu/forsec/Filson.html.

Fink, Sheri. "Saving Eden." *Discover* 26, no. 7 (July 2005): pp. 54–59.

Gosner, Kenneth L. *Atlantic Seashore: A Field Guide to Sponges, Jellyfish, Sea Urchins, and More*. New York: Houghton Mifflin Company, 1978.

Gunderson, Lance H. "Ecological Resilience—In Theory and Application." *Annual Review of Ecology and Systematics* 31 (2000): pp. 425–439.

International Mire Conservation Group. "Wetland Restoration in Iraq." Available online at: http://www.imcg.net/imcgnl/n10105/Kap09.htm.

Jacono, C. C. "Giant Salvinia." USGS. 2003. Available online at: http://salvinia.er.usgs.gov/html/identification.html.

King County Department of Natural Resources and Parks. "Best Management Practices: Giant Hogweed." Available online at: http://dnr.metrokc.gov/weeds.

Koch, Maryjo. *Pond, Lake, River, Sea*. San Francisco: Swan Island Books, 1994.

Margulis, Lynn. *Symbiotic Planet*. Amherst, Mass.: Basic Books, 1998.

Martin, M. R., and C. Stiles. "The Use of Hand-harvesting to Control Eurasian Milfoil in Upper Saranac Lake, Franklin County, NY." Presentation at the NEAPMS annual conference, Saratoga Springs, N.Y., 2005.

Randall, J. M., and J. Marinelli. *Invasive Plants: Weeds of the Global Garden*. Brooklyn, N.Y.: Brooklyn Botanic Gardens Publications, 1996.

Singleton, J.R. "Production and Utilization of Waterfowl Food Plants on the East Texas Gulf Coast." *Journal of Wildlife Management* 15, no. 1 (1951): pp. 46–56.

Silvertown, Jonathan. "Plant Phenotypic Plasticity and Non-cognitive Behaviour." *Trends in Ecology and Evolution* 13 (1998): pp. 255–256.

Sprenger, Matthew D., Loren Smith, and John P. Taylor. "Testing Control of Saltcedar Seedlings Using Fall Flooding." *Wetlands* 21, no. 3 (2001): pp. 437–441.

Thompson, D.Q., and R.L. Stuckey. "Spread, Impact, and Control of Purple Loosestrife (*Lythrum Salicaria*) in North American Wetlands. The Case for Biological Control." USGS. Available online at http://www.npwrc.usgs.gov/resource/plants/loosstrf.htm

University of Florida, Center for Aquatic and Invasive Plants. "Water Hyacinth *Eichhornia crassipes*." Available online at: http://plants.ifas.ufl.edu/hyacin.html.

Washington State Department of Ecology. "Non-native Freshwater Plants Giant Hogweed." Available online at: http://www.ecy.wa.gov/programs/wq/plants/weeds/aqua012.html.

Washington State Department of Ecology. "Non-native Freshwater Plants Reed Canarygrass." Available online at http://www.ecy.wa.gov/programs/wq/plants/weeds/aqua011.html.

Wilson, E.O. *The Diversity of Life*. Cambridge, Mass.: Belknap Press of Harvard University, 1992.

# FURTHER READING

Baskin, Y. *A Plague of Rats and Rubbervines: The Growing Threat of Species Invasions.* Covelo, Calif.: Shearwater Books, 2003.

Coombs, E.M., J.K. Clark, G.L. Piper, and A.F. Cofrancesco Jr. *Biological Control of Invasive Plants in the United States.* Corvallis: Oregon State University, 2004.

Cox, G. *Alien Species and Evolution: The Evolutionary Ecology of Exotic Plants, Animals, Microbes, and Interacting Native Species.* Washington, D.C.: Island Press, 2004.

Cronk, J.K., and M.S. Fennessy. *Wetland Plants: Biology and Ecology.* Boca Raton, Fla.: CRC Press, 2001.

DiTomaso, J.M. *Aquatic and Riparian Weeds of the West.* Collingdale, Pa.: DIANE Publishing Company, 2003.

Mooney, H.A. *Invasive Species in a Changing World.* Washington, D.C.: Island Press, 2000.

Randall, J.M. and J. Marinelli. *Invasive Plants: Weeds of the Global Garden.* Brooklyn, N.Y.: Brooklyn Botanic Gardens Publications, 1996.

Wilson, E.O. *The Diversity of Life.* Cambridge, Mass.: Belknap Press of Harvard University, 1992.

Wilson, E.O. *The Future of Life.* New York: Vintage Publishing, 2003.

Witson, T. *Weeds of the West, 9th ed.* Collingdale, Pa.: DIANE Publishing Company, 2000.

Zimdahl, R. *Fundamentals of Weed Science, 2nd ed.* New York: Academic Press, 1998.

## WEB SITES

**Center for Invasive Plant Management**
http://www.weedcenter.org

**The Federal Aquatic Nuisance Species Task Force**
http://anstaskforce.gov/default.php

**The Federal Interagency Committee for the Management of
    Noxious and Exotic Weeds**
http://www.fws.gov/ficmnew

**Florida Department of Environmental Protection**
http://www.dep.state.fl.us/lands/invaspec

**Invasive Species in the Great Lakes Region**
http://www.great-lakes.net/envt/flora-fauna/invasive/invasive.html

**National Park Service—Invasive Species Management**
http://www.nature.nps.gov/biology/invasivespecies

**National Park Service—"Weeds Gone Wild"**
http://www.nps.gov/plants/alien/moreinfo.htm

**U.S. National Arboretum**
http://www.usna.usda.gov/Gardens/invasives.html

**USDA—Animal and Plant Health Inspection Service (APHIS)**
http://www.aphis.usda.gov

**USDA—InvasiveSpecies Information Center**
http://www.invasivespeciesinfo.gov

**USDA—Natural Resources Conservation Service (NRCS)**
http://www.pwrc.usgs.gov/WLI/wris1.htm

**USDA/NRCS Plants Database**
http://plants.nrcs.usda.gov/cgi_bin/noxious.cgi?earl=noxious.cgi

# PICTURE CREDITS

# INDEX

## ABOUT THE AUTHOR

**Suellen May** writes for agricultural and environmental publications. She is a graduate of the University of Vermont (B.S.) and Colorado State University (M.S.). She has worked in the environmental field for 15 years, including in invasive species management for Larimer County Parks and Open Lands in Colorado. She served as the Education Committee chairperson for the Colorado Weed Management Association. While living in Fort Collins, Colorado, she founded the Old Town Writers' Group, which continues to thrive. She lives with her son, Nate, in Bucks County, Pennsylvania. Readers can reach her at suellen0829@yahoo.com.